ALEXANDER GALICH SONGS & POEMS

Translated & Edited by
Gerald Stanton Smith

Ardis, Ann Arbor

Alexander Galich, *Songs and Poems*
Edited and translated by Gerald Stanton Smith
Copyright © *1983 by Ardis Publishers*
All rights reserved
Printed in the United States of America
No part of this publication may be
reproduced, stored in a retrieval system
or transmitted in any form or by any means,
electronic, mechanical, photocopying, recording,
or otherwise, without the prior permission
of the publisher

Ardis Publishers
2901 Heatherway
Ann Arbor, Michigan 48104

ISBN 0-88233-952-4 (cloth)

Library of Congress Cataloging in Publication Data

Galich, Aleksandr, 1919-
Songs and poems.

Includes bibliographical references.
I. Smith, Gerry. II. Title.
PG3476.G34A27   1983   891.71'42   83-15524
ISBN 0-88233-952-4

For I. Z. and R. A.

Contents

Acknowledgments

The translations of *Fame is the Spur, Goldminers' Waltz, How Klim Petrovich Protested . . ., The Transmigration of Souls, Warning,* and *Hospital Gypsy Song* were first published in *Index on Censorship*, III, 3 (1974). The cycle *An Attempt at Nostalgia* appeared in *Kontinent I: The Alternative Voice of Russia and Eastern Europe* (London, Andre Deutsch, 1976).

I would like to thank Tanya Chambers, Anne Cluysenaar, and Viktor and Marina Raskin for their help and advice at various times. Vladimir Frumkin transcribed the musical examples, and I am very grateful to him for permission to use them as well as for his assistance with points of detail.

I owe a special debt of gratitude to Martin Dewhirst and Michael Nicholson for sharing with me their unique knowledge of Russian sources.

Work on this book was completed during my tenure of a Research Fellowship in the University of Liverpool, and I am grateful to Professor A. B. McMillin for his advice and support.

G. S.

Alexander Galich

Songs and Poems

Silence Is Connivance: Alexander Galich

Moscow's Lord Fauntleroy

Lev Kopelev, who was to become a close friend of Alexander Galich when both men were in their forties and fifties, wrote the following description of him as he was in his teens:

> He used to be Sasha Ginzburg, a boy from a Moscow intelligentsia family—Little Lord Fauntleroy from Krivokolennyi Lane. He was excellent at school, could declaim with expression, write poetry, play the piano, sing old parlour love songs and revolutionary songs; he was a good dancer and a favorite with boys and girls alike.[1]

The pen name "Galich," which he used throughout his literary career, is made up from the initial of his real surname, the first syllable of his given name, and the final syllable of his (and almost every other) patronymic: Ginzburg, Alexander Arkadevich. Besides being the name of an ancient Russian town, Galich was also the name of one of Pushkin's schoolteachers and is immortalized in his poetry. There is one near parallel to Galich's choice; another of Pushkin's friends, the famous rake Kaverin, had his name adopted by the novelist Veniamin Alexandrovich Zilber, born in 1902, who came to fame in the 1930s.[2]

Galich was born in Ekaterinoslav (now Dniepropetrovsk) on 19 October 1919; some official sources give the year of his birth as 1918. His childhood years were spent in Sevastopol, Rostov-on-Don, Baku and other towns in the south of Russia before his family moved finally to Moscow in the mid-1920s. One of his uncles on his father's side was a professor of Russian literature at Moscow University, and this connection played a decisive part in Galich's life. By chance, when they moved to Moscow from the south his parents settled in a house that in the early nineteenth century had belonged to the family of the poet Dmitri Venevitinov; and in one room of this house, a room which after the revolution had been divided into no less than four flats, one of which was occupied by Galich's family, Pushkin had given the first reading of *Boris Godunov.* The centenary of this event, in 1926, was commemorated by a select gathering in the room, with lectures by prominent Pushkinists, among them Galich's uncle, and readings from Pushkin's works by some of the leading actors of the day, including such great figures as Kachalov and Leonidov. Galich tells the story of this evening in his autobiographical book *The Dress Rehearsal,* and says that as a result he became "theater crazy."[3]

However, he was to begin his higher education in a literary rather than a theatrical institute. He had begun writing poetry in his early teens, and in the normal Soviet way had been drafted into the lower depths of official literary circles as a member of the group for aspiring young writers attached to the newspaper of the childrens' organization, *Pionerskaia pravda;* the adolescent Galich published poetry both there and in its companion journal, *Pioner.* Again in the normal Soviet fashion, consultations were arranged for the young poets with senior professionals, and Galich thereby came to have his work discussed by Ilia Selvinsky, Boris Lugovskoy, and Mikhail Svetlov, all of them front-rank Soviet poets at the time. The senior poet he remembered with most affection, however, was Eduard Bagritsky (1896-1934); Bagritsky actually mentioned Galich's work favorably in print, and with this recommendation behind him, Galich entered the poetry department of the Moscow Literary Institute in 1935.

The chance of an entree into Galich's original preference, the theater, became a reality when in 1935 he was successful in a fiercely competitive examination for a place in the first intake of students for what was to prove the last pedagogical venture in the career of the great director Konstantin Stanislavsky. After a frantic year during which he studied at both institutions simultaneously, he abandoned his course at the Literary Institute and opted finally for the Stanislavsky Studio of Opera and Drama. For four years he was trained by Stanislavsky and his associates. This experience had a comic side as well as the obvious advantages. Stanislavsky's none-too-inspiring relatives made up approximately one third of the teaching staff, and they gave courses that the students thought irrelevant and old-fashioned. Galich subsequently realized that not a single one of all the carefully chosen students ever became a first-rate professional actor; he judged that this was because he and his fellows were being trained, not for the actual theater as it existed in reality, but for some "Temple of the Theater" that existed in Stanislavsky's ageing mind. Galich was among the guinea pigs for Stanislavsky's final experiment, the "theory of physical actions," according to which, as Galich summarized it, "the correct physical actions should bring the player to correct deportment, correct deportment should evoke the correct frame of mind, and the correct frame of mind should help him find the correct words."[4] So Galich "rehearsed" *Hamlet* for weeks, under strict instructions not to learn the words, which were supposed to "evolve" as the actors developed the characters through their physical actions.

But at the same time, of course, this temple of eccentricity brought Galich into contact with what remained of the great Moscow Arts Theater of pre-revolutionary times. Besides Stanislavsky himself, there was Olga Knipper, Chekhov's widow; and on special occasions the greatest living actors such as Moskvin and Kachalov would come and take part in the Studio's activities. Galich's particular favorite among the older actor-instructors was that same Leonidov whom he had heard reciting Pushkin in his parents' flat in 1926. But all this came to an end with Stanislavsky's death in August 1938; the Studio simply disintegrated.

Apart from the incidents he chose to mention in *The Dress Rehearsal*, Galich divulged little of his personal life, and especially little about his life before the 1960s. In 1977, in the course of the last interview he ever gave, however, he allowed himself to reminisce about the destruction of cultural values he had witnessed in the 1930s:

> I remember that in 1936 I was present at the last performance given by the Moscow Art Theater No. 2 Company. This was the theater that the intelligentsia loved most, maybe even more than Moscow Arts Theater No. 1. The decree concerning its closure was published one morning, and the last performance took place that evening. Through a farcical concatenation of circumstances, the play that evening was Duval's *Prayer for Life.* It's a comedy. But it was played to hollow sobs from the audience. And when the play finished there was a genuine demonstration: for nearly fifteen minutes the audience stood and applauded; they would not leave. And remember that those were terrible years—arrests, purges and trials. But the audience stood for fifteen minutes seeing its favorite theater off into oblivion ...[5]

Galich also mentioned in the same interview that he witnessed the demolition of some of Moscow's oldest churches in the 1930s, including the Shrine of Christ the Savior with its priceless Nesterov frescoes. However, as Galich said in *The Dress Rehearsal,* the terrible saturnalia that was in full swing round about them was felt by the teenaged actors in Stanislavsky's Studio to have nothing whatsoever to do with them; they lived "in an invented, unreal, illusory world."[6] Raisa Orlova, a friend of Galich since their childhood, remembered the dashing Galich of these years:

> ... I can see the flat of my childhood, on Gorky Street, where the handsome Sasha Ginzburg, who didn't know yet what he would do—write poetry or paint pictures, compose music or be an actor, Sasha, gripped by the foretaste of fame, used to sit at our broken-down piano and sing, and we would join in: "My Masha and I by the samovar," "Bottles and glasses on the table," "There's a reason why fate gave us the wine of love" ...[7]

And Galich's near-contemporary, the novelist Viktor Nekrasov, reminisced in much the same vein after Galich's death:

> I knew Sasha since about forty years ago, maybe more. We were both young then, and we were dreaming about the theater and had no doubt that we could "burn peoples' hearts." Sasha had already made friends with his guitar and could sing songs nicely, but when

one looked at him, so handsome and soulful, and envied him a bit (he'd been accepted by the Stanislavsky studio and I hadn't), did anyone think then, could anyone have imagined, that he would "burn peoples' hearts" not from the stage of the Moscow Arts Theater, but in a completely different way . . .[8]

When the Stanislavsky studio fell to pieces after the great man's death, Galich transferred to the Moscow Theatrical Studio, which was just beginning to come together under the leadership of two aspiring young men, the dramatist Aleksei Arbuzov and the director V. N. Pluchek. The majority of the participants in the venture were still in their teens. The flagwaving project with which the studio launched its public existence was a collectively developed drama about the city of Komsomolsk-na-Amure. This city was built up on the basis of the old town of Permskoe by volunteer members of the Komsomol, beginning in 1932; it is situated on the Amur river in the far east of Siberia, about 200 miles north-east of Khabarovsk. In the Soviet mythology of the 1930s it was heavily promoted as the youth movement's contribution to the great task of industrialization and modernization undertaken in the Five-Year Plans. The words of a Soviet history of the theater tell the story best:

> In their striving to recreate an authentic picture of the construction of the Komsomol city, to convey the unique atmosphere of heroic creation, the members of the Studio read deeply in Komsomol newspapers, entered into correspondence with the residents of Komsomolsk, and lost no opportunity for discussion with people visiting from there.
> Every part in the play was conceived by the actor playing it, and he put into it his experience of life, his most ardent hopes and dreams. The dramatic relations between the characters arose and were developed during the course of mass rehearsals. Arbuzov, Gerdt, Gladkov and Kuznetsov selected the most successful ones from among them and created a preliminary scenario. Pluchek was in charge of the rehearsals. The improvised text, taken down by special secretaries during the rehearsals, was reworked and polished many times by Arbuzov. In this way the "dramatic chronicle" *City of the Dawn* was created.[9]

In its final form, the play had some innovatory and experimental features. It gave unusual prominence to mass scenes, and paid little attention to the detailed development of characters; the action proceeded by means of short episodes connected by speeches from a chorus of Komsomols, who commented on the action, engaged the characters in dialogue, and also directly addressed the audience. The play had its first night in February 1941. Galich was one of the principal actors and therefore authors; he played "the Komsomol leader Borshchagovsky, whom the reinforced-concrete Old Bolshevik Bagrov and the other "good" Komsomols unmask as a covert Trotskyite. At the end of the play I leave for Moscow where, it is quite obvious, I will be arrested."[10]

After *City of the Dawn* had been launched, Galich joined up with two of his fellow juniors from the company, Isai Kuznetsov and Vsevolod Bagritsky (the son of the poet) and wrote his first play, *The Duel*. This play was put into rehearsal, and had its first try-out on 21 June 1941; the German invasion the next day put an end to this and all the other activities of the Studio.

Galich was rejected for military service on medical grounds. At a loose end, he joined a geological expedition to the North Caucasus, but the expedition split up in the oil city of Grozny, the capital of the Chechen-Ingush Autonomous Republic. Here Galich became director of the municipal theater and began writing plays and songs for their shows. In 1942, when the city was threatened by the advancing German armies (it was at this time that Stalin ordered the deportation to Siberia of the entire Chechen-Ingush nation along with several others regarded as potential collaborators), Galich made his way to the town of Chirchik to join the rump of his former colleagues from the Moscow Theatrical Studio, now led by Pluchek alone; the group reformed as a forces entertainment troupe, and Galich spent the rest of the war as a member of this company, travelling far and wide around the fronts, and undertaking the most varied activities as writer and actor.

Among these activities was the composition and performance to guitar accompaniment of *chastushki,* the four-line form that is standard in Russian for impromptu humorous or satirical rhymes. In *The Dress Rehearsal* Galich remembers doing this on hospital trains:

> With my throat itching from the sweetish smell of carbolic, iodine, and congealed blood, I would read from *Graf Nulin* and sing *chastushki* to my guitar. I used to make them up on the spot as I went along, after a preliminary chat with the commissar or the train commander. These *chastushki* were very unsophisticated, but they mentioned the names of the wounded and the medical personnel, and described real events, usually funny ones, and because of this they always had an undeservedly roaring success.[11]

After the war Galich returned to Moscow and set about making a career as a dramatist. He was to meet with considerable success; in the ten years after 1945 he wrote or co-wrote a number of plays that were widely performed. This period has been described as "the nadir of the Soviet theater," when the grim atmosphere of fear, uncertainty and cowardice stifled any attempt at creative originality. Authors were cowed into writing feeble plays which were no more that hortatory lantern-lectures to illustrate the latest twist in the zig-zagging party line . . . Matters reached the depth of absurdity when one of the most compliant Soviet playwrights, Nikolai Virta, propounded the theory of "lack of conflict." According to his, the only possible basis of drama for a Soviet play was the struggle between the 'good' and the 'better'.[12]

Things reached such an embarrassing level of stagnation that even before the relaxation of literary life that followed Stalin's death in 1953, the Party organization within the Moscow branch of the Union of Writers initiated a discussion of the problems of the theater, with special reference to comedy. The result was a symposium published in the professional journal *Theater (Teatr);* Virta's "no conflict" theory was condemned as a reason for the writers' lack of success. But there were even bolder suggestions. The critic M. Nikonov also asserted that "authors should not consent to revise a play *against their conscience and inner convictions.*" This sentence must have stimulated some ghoulish smiles among the dramatists of the time. It is interesting, though, that the example Nikonov picked to illustrate a play ruined because of its author's spinelessness in agreeing to alterations was *Moscow Does Not Believe in Tears (Moskva slezam ne verit),* which Galich had written in 1949 in co-authorship with the established scenarist and short-story writer Georgii Munblit.[13] Galich never mentioned this episode in his public statements, and what degree of time-serving and compromise was involved in this play, as in his others that were performed, we shall probably never know.

Galich's reputation as a playwright was established by the first work of his to be staged after the war. It was not the first play he had written after his war service; as we shall see, the latter was *Sailor's Rest (Matrosskaia tishina),* which Galich conceived in the spring of 1945 but then set aside because of its obvious lack of accord with the prevailing literary atmosphere. His first play to be staged was a vaudeville called *Taimyr' Calling (Vas vyzyvaet Taimyr').* The vaudeville was regarded as a particularly disaster-prone area in post-war Soviet theater, and the lack of a viable repertoire opened the door to instant success for anyone who could produce something ideologically tolerable that even approached playability. *Taimyr' Calling* was written by Galich in collaboration with Konstantin Isaev (b.1907), a film scenarist who had been active in literature since the mid-1930s. The Taimyr' is a peninsula and also river in northwest Siberia. In the play,

almost all the people are positive. They get into an amusing mélange of events and misunderstandings. The result is a very funny, witty piece in which the authors, with commendable inventiveness, tell the story of how Diuzhnikov stays behind in a room of the Hotel Moscow waiting for a phone call from Taimyr', and mixes up all the commissions given him by the other people who live in the room. Since there are no negative characters in the play, the authors have to rely on the "mechanics" of the plot, in which comic situations show positive people in a comic light. The result, inevitably, is that the authors had to go over the top with misunderstandings and confusions, and the characters turn out to be too much at the mercy of the twists and turns of the plot.[14]

Despite these obvious deficiencies, the play was staged for many years all over the USSR and in the socialist countries, adapted for radio and broadcast numerous times. It was even played by the left-wing Unity Theater in London in 1956. The play established Galich as a Soviet writer, and his career as such continued to build through the 1950s; it was at its highest point towards the end of that decade. In 1958, "in honor of the fortieth anniversary of the Komsomol," Galich wrote a "romantic comedy in three acts," *The Name of the Ship is "Eagle" (Parokhod zovut "Orlenok")*; its text was published in the prestigious series *Contemporary Drama*.[15] The text was prefaced by a drawing of Galich in black shirt and white tie, with neatly trimmed moustache and hair just beginning to recede, and a biographical note that makes him sound like the model Soviet writer for young people; it mentions his contributions to the Pioneer publications before the war, his war effort, a play called *Street of Boys (Ulitsa mal'chikov)*, dated to 1946 and said to be his first play, but not mentioned anywhere else in the available literature on Galich. One other detail mentioned in this account is that Galich "wrote the texts of a number of popular Soviet songs: *Goodbye, Mummy, Don't be Sad (Do svidan'ia, mama, ne goriui)*, with music by V. I. Solov'ev-Sedoi; *Oh, Northern Sea (Oi ty, Severnoe more)*, with music by M. I. Blanter; *Run Along, Run Along, Road (Ty begi, begi, doroga)*, with music by A. Ia. Lepin, and others." The final accolade in this note is the last sentence, which informs the reader that Galich "is now working on a chronicle play called *Communists, Forward (Kommunisty, vpered)*."

A chance encounter with the rising Galich of 1951, now a Beau Brummell rather than a Little Lord Fauntleroy, was worked into an autobiographical novel published nearly 25 years later by Vladimir Maximov:

It was on the corner of Mokhovaya and Gorky Street, outside the main entrance of the National Hotel, amid a crowd that was colorful yet pathetic in its pretensions, that Vlad remembers seeing a man with a dandyish cane under his arm. Wearing a light-colored overcoat, this tall, handsome creature with a luxuriant moustache and a halo of flowing, carefully tended hair moved through the crowd like a visitor from a dream, an emissary of Sheherezade, a vision from another, unearthly world, and the aroma of his well-groomed cleanliness floated behind him like a scarf of the finest material.

You and he will meet again, Sasha Galich, only it will be almost twenty years later, in other surroundings and in very different circumstances, and it is to be hoped that you will both regret that the meeting did not take place earlier.[16]

The official career of Galich is summarized in the 1961 *Theatrical Encyclopedia;* besides the events and plays already mentioned, it mentions *Under a Lucky Star (Pod schastlivoi zvezdoiu),* performed by the Theater of the Leningrad Soviet in 1954; *Campaign March (Pokhodnyi marsh),* performed by the New Theater, Leningrad, in 1957; and *Does a Man Need Much? (Mnogo li nuzhno cheloveku?),* played at the Vakhtangov Theater, Moscow, in 1959.[17] Of these, *Campaign March* is another anniversary play for the Komsomol, this time written in verse. The *Encyclopedia* says in conclusion that "the central theme of Galich's work is the romance of the struggle and the creative labor of Soviet youth."[18] The *Concise Literary Encyclopedia,* the relevant volume of which was published in 1964, gives the details of Galich's plays, and comments: "Galich's comedies are characterized by romantic elevation, lyricism, and humor. Galich is the author of popular songs about youth."[19]

Galich made his debut as a scriptwriter for the cinema in 1951, with a film called *In the Steppes (V stepi);* between then and 1967 he wrote or co-wrote at least eight films. Two of them were particularly successful; *The State Criminal (Gosudarstvennyi prestupnik,* 1964), which won an award from the Ministry of Internal Affairs, and *She Who Runs across the Waves (Begush-chaia po volnam,* 1967), based on the novel by the interesting Soviet writer of fantasy literature, Alexander Grin (1880-1932). He also wrote screenplays for cartoons and the texts for several songs that were used in films.[20] As a result of his efforts in the cinema industry, Galich received the significant accolade, bestowed at the time on very few and very trustworthy individuals, of being the Soviet representative in joint international cultural projects. With Paul Andrest he co-wrote the script for a Franco-Soviet film called *Third Youth (Tret'ia molodost'),* about the life of the balletmaster Marius Petipa, and in this connection made two visits to Paris without the usual massive "delegation"; and he also visited Norway on film business, making connections that were later to prove very useful.

All these various activities made Galich a member of the Moscow literary elite. He was

...one of the top dozen Moscow scriptwriters and drama-
tists ... Sasha was a member of every possible union, society,
committee, section. He had awards, diplomas and so on. Sasha
was enchanting, witty, and handsome, he loved elegant foreign-
looking clothes, he used to travel abroad. He was a fine piano
player, a king at billiards and a first-rate preference and poker
player. Sasha lived well, had no lack of money, and had a
magnificent flat in the writers' apartment building near Aeroflo-
tovskaia underground station, and in it I've seen quite a few
antiques.[21]

This was Galich as remembered by an acquaintance, the writer Iury Krotkov,
at what was to prove the turning point of his life; in his early forties, Galich
embarked upon a new kind of literary activity that was eventually to take away
his hard-earned and well-loved livelihood. In or around 1962, he began
writing and performing songs that had no hope of being accepted by the
literary world he had seemed to fit into so comfortably.

The Shitometer

Why and how did this prosperous and apparently well-adapted Soviet
playwright turn into an underground poet?

To begin with, not everything during Galich's years of acceptance was
part of a joyful journey onward and upward towards literary success. From
common knowledge of the Soviet literary process, especially when Galich was
beginning as a dramatist, and from the evidence of Nikonov's article that was
referred to earlier, we know that there must have been constant circum-
spection and compromise on his part. And Galich was later to mention two
particular events, separated by a decade, that brought him into confrontation
with the hard facts of Soviet literary life.

In 1948 and 1949 there had been the notorious campaign against
"cosmopolitans," the euphemism employed at the time to refer to Jews, in
Soviet cultural and intellectual life; there was a wholesale purge of Jews from
these spheres. Among the most prominent victims was the great actor and
director Solomon Mikhailovich Mikhoels, who had been artistic director of
the State Yiddish Theater in Moscow since 1929; he was murdered by the
secret police in Minsk in 1948. Galich saw Mikhoels in his office the day before
he went on his last journey; Mikhoels showed him some documentary
materials about the wartime rising in the Warsaw ghetto.[22] After Mikhoels'
disappearance, for reasons that he did not comprehend himself, Galich felt
impelled to try and take part in the work of the Yiddish section of the Moscow
Union of Writers, even though he did not know a word of the language. He
went to the next meeting of the section after Mikhoels' death. The poet Perets

Markish, who was in the chair at the meeting, found the opportunity to confront Galich and tell him rudely to clear off. Galich left, feeling hurt and offended. But then two weeks later almost the entire membership of the Yiddish section was arrested; and many of them, including Markish, were shot. Galich concluded his account of this incident: "And now I know that Markish, at the very moment that he publicly called me "an alien" and threw me out of the meeting, was doing no less than saving my life, the life of a silly little boy."[23]

Ten years later, at the end of 1958, Galich had what appears to have been his first really serious clash with the literary authorities. At issue was his play *Sailor's Rest (Matrosskaia tishina*—the title is the name of a street in Moscow). Galich used the text and banning of this play as the center around which he built his only autobiographical work in prose, *The Dress Rehearsal,* which was written in 1973, and published abroad the following year. Galich had conceived and begun writing this play in the spring of 1945, inspired by the enthusiasm and patriotism of those heady days of victory and national solidarity. The play centers on the relationships between three generations of a Russian Jewish family; there is the father, Abram Shvarts, his son David, and David's son, also called David. The play is in four acts, set successively in the mid-1920s, 1937, 1944, and 1955. At the start of the play, Abram, a struggling petty entrepreneur, focuses his ambitions on his son, sometimes even using physical force to make him practice the violin; David has genuine talent, though, and goes up to the Moscow Conservatoire just before the war. He wins a state competition and seems set to become a star musician. But the war comes, he becomes a junior officer, is wounded and eventually dies in a hospital; before his death, as he is being transported on a hospital train, he has a vision of his father's ghost. Old Abram tells his son how he was shot dead after slapping a Gestapo officer during a particularly insulting incident during the deportation of Jews from the ghetto in their native town of Tulchin. Old resentments are defused and father and son are reconciled. But David has had a son by his childhood sweetheart Tania; in the fourth act of the play, this second David and his mother wonder what the future holds for them. They are visited by another childhood friend of David and Tania, Hannah, who brings her son from her marriage to Skorobogatenko, a sea captain based in the Far East. David and Hannah are Jewish, and Tania and Skorobogatenko Russian and Ukrainian respectively. The point of the play, as Galich himself described it, was "to demonstrate that in Soviet Russia for representatives of Jewish nationality (Galich uses the official phrase) the path of assimilation is not only sensible, but is the most natural, normal, and regular path."[24] The Jews in the play come to feel themselves to be equal citizens with the Russians and have the right to call the USSR "My Great Country," as violinist David's dying words put it. Naturally, the events of the late 1940s that were mentioned earlier meant that there could be no question of the play being finished and submitted for performance then; but in the more relaxed atmosphere of the late 1950s, "after the XX Congress of the Party and Khrushchev's unmasking Stalin's crimes . . . Once more we started believing! Once more, like sheep we bleated with joy and rushed out into the nice green grass—which turned out to be a stinking bog!"[25]

Galich finished the play during the Thaw and gave some private readings of it, but did not submit it formally to a theater for performance; he was approached by Mikhail Kozakov and Oleg Efremov, who got wind of it and wanted to use it as one of the premiere pieces for the Sovremennik Theater in Moscow, which at the time was just in the process of formation. The play went into production, but the Party authorities made sure by covert instruction that it would never be performed publicly, at the Sovremennik or anywhere else. This decision must have been a severe blow to Galich's self-respect and professional pride; for at the time, literary works that seemed rather more objectionable than his play were being published and performed. The process that was to culminate in the publication of *One Day in the Life of Ivan Denisovich* in 1962 was—though always with steps back and hesitations—in spate.

About a fortnight after the mockery of his play's dress rehearsal, Galich obtained an interview at Party headquarters to discuss the reasons why the play could not be permitted to have public performance. The interview was granted by a certain Sokolova, one of the two Party representatives, both women, who had attended the dress rehearsal. Her words, as reported by Galich, were astonishingly blunt:

> Well, Comrade Galich, so that's what you'd like—in the middle of the capital city, in a new central theater, there should be a play telling the story of how the Jews won the war?! They're all Jews!

And she went on to make the message even more crude:

> I admit that the Jewish people suffered greatly in the war, it's true! But other peoples suffered no less. And it was only the Russians, Ukrainians and Belorussians who took up arms to defend their territory . . . And what did the Jews do? They went like . . . they went humbly to the slaughter . . . without resistance. A tragedy? Yes! But for a Russian, Alexander Ar-ka-di-e-vich, in this tragedy there is something profoundly degrading and shameful . . .[26]

This experience, and the more open anti-semitism that followed the Six Day War and the beginning of Jewish repatriation from the USSR, fuelled some of Galich's most bitter songs and undoubtedly played a significant part in his disillusionment with his position as a Soviet writer in good standing.

It would be wrong to think of Galich's "rebirth" as a single, once-for-all-time decision. For some years, in the mid-1960s, he was leading a double life, writing dissident songs and at the same time earning high fees for his film scripts and other writing contracts. As Orlova says:

> Galich didn't want an evil fate for himself, and he wasn't prepared for suffering. But all the more courageous it was that he did not step on the throat of his own song. After all, when he was starting out, when his songs had flown around Moscow and then through the country, and then abroad,—there wasn't the slightest notion of emigration, the PEN Club of France, the possibility of a different choice . . . If he had been a different personality,—nearer to the sacred image, the icon,—then his extraordinary songs would not exist.[27]

There was thus, apparently, an increasing contradiction that Galich felt between the targets he was attacking in his songs and the way he himself was living. One remarkable aspect of this was that while his songs more often than not spoke from the point of view of the "victims," Galich and everyone who knew him were well aware that he had not been one of them. But like practically everyone else in the USSR, he had a close relative who had suffered repression:

> His brother had been in the camps. I thought that during the Thaw Sasha was even a bit jealous of him. But probably what he felt much more strongly was relief that it hadn't happened to him, that the shells had fallen into other craters.[28]

Galich himself spoke about this factor in an interview given soon after he arrived in the West. It turns out that the person concerned was actually not his sibling, but a cousin (*dvoiurodnyi brat*):

> If I can speak more frankly, I had a cousin. He was closer than my immediate family, he brought me up. I'm obliged to him that I learned to read and got interested in anything in life . . . He spent 24 years there; I never forgot him and suffered infinitely for him.[29]

When Galich turned to the composition of satirical songs, then, he was at least in part condemning the system under which he had grown up, Stalinism. This target was sanctioned by Khrushchev's "Secret Speech" of 1956. But there was more to it than this. Galich turned with particular and increasing vehemence against the specific professional environment in which he had been formed, against those writers and artists who remained within the fold. Their reaction was one of bewilderment:

24

But he's ours, one of us. As for Litvinov and Bukovsky, or even
Sakharov and Solzhenitsyn,—they come from a different world.
We've never seen them. But Sashka? I know him through and
through. Him an unmasker? Him a fighter for truth? It's a laugh,
and it's a sin . . . [30]

Galich probably came closest to spelling out his objections to the official world
of literature when speaking not about himself, but about the leading director
Georgy Tovstonogov; he had reached a prominent position in the theatrical
world, thanks to his gifts, energy, and even a certain courage, but

It's one thing to make one's way up. To stay there is quite another
thing. No creative gift, no kind of energy, or even less courage can
help you in that. And there begins the shameful path of
compromises, bargains with your own conscience, calculations
like: OK, I'll put on this shit-awful play for such-and-such an
anniversary or solemn historical date, but then after that . . .

And this cherished "after that" never comes, it never will
come; so talent fades, energy runs out, and even the very word
"courage" disappears forever from your vocabulary. [31]

Galich summed it all up when in 1975 in Washington he said to Iury Krotkov:

D'you know why I did all that? Because I was sick of serving. You
know what I mean. Back there in Russia, a writer has to
serve . . . [32]

The vestiges of service remained for some time, performed with increasing
reluctance and accepted with increasing ill grace. Galich helped to write a
dramatic script from Iury Trifonov's novel *Slaking the Thirst (Utolenie
zhazhdy)*, and it was put on by the Moscow Arts Theater, having its premiere
in March 1966. [33] The same theater premiered a play co-written by Galich with
I. Grekova, the highly regarded short-story writer, *Weekdays and Holidays
(Budni i prazdniki)* on 19 September 1967; [34] Galich does not mention this
piece either in *The Dress Rehearsal* or in any other personal statement,
probably because Grekova remained in the USSR and showed no sign of
wanting to become involved in dissident activity, although her stories have
been fairly widely published and discussed outside the country.

The earliest "publication" of Galich's songs came in the collection
Sphinxes (Sfinksy), one of the pioneering *samizdat* literary collections of the
1960s; it was published by the group calling themselves *SMOG* (in Russian,
the initials stand either for "Courage, Thought, Image, Profundity," or
alternatively "The Youngest Society of Geniuses"). [35] The contributors to this
collection were on the whole much younger than Galich, and whether he

25

himself had any knowledge of the publication before the event is unknown, but unlikely. Four songs were included: *Clouds (Oblaka)*, *My Friends Are Going Away (Ukhodiat druz'ia)*, the song that has now become immortal under the title *Goldminer's Waltz (Staratel'skii val'sok)*, here entitled *Silence is Gold (Molchanie—zoloto)*, and the song later called *Warning (Predosterezhenie)*, here called *Jewish Domestic Song (Domashniaia evreiskaia)*. This collection rapidly made its way abroad, and was published in *Grani (Facets)*, the literary journal of the anti-Soviet political organization NTS, based in Frankfurt-on-Main.[36] This publication was followed by more songs in the same journal the following year. For a Soviet writer, to have his work appear in this journal was and remains a matter for very serious concern: it is officially taken to mean either that the writer sent it himself, and thereby committed an act of open treachery, or that the editors of the most dedicated anti-Soviet journal considered the writer's work sufficiently sympathetic to their cause to find space for it. Galich responded to the beginning of these publications by trying to defend himself: a copy of *Grani* containing his work that mysteriously appeared in his mailbox was immediately delivered by him to the Executive Secretary of the Union of Writers, Viktor Il'in (well known to be a general in the KGB), and protestations made that the author had nothing to do with the publication.[37]

The pivotal point in Galich's relations with the Soviet literary authorities came in the course of 1968. It witnessed his greatest triumph as a poet-singer, a performance at the now legendary "Festival of Bards" that took place before an audience of two and a half thousand people in March in the Siberian city of Akademgorodok, a new city populated almost entirely by scientific research workers engaged at the institutes nearby. At this concert Galich performed his *Pasternak In Memoriam,* and the reception of this song remained for him one of the three "blessed moments" of his life that he enumerated in *The Dress Rehearsal:*

> The auditorium of the House of Scientists in Akademgorodok in Novosibirsk. As I now realize, this was my first and last open concert, with tickets even being sold for it.
> I had just finished performing my *Pasternak in Memoriam,* and behold, after the final words, something improbable happened—the audience, two thousand-odd people that evening, rose to its feet and for a whole moment stood in silence before breaking out in tumultous applause.[38]

Raisa Orlova thought that in his description of this incident Galich

> probably underestimated it. Our friends in Akademgorodok told us that the people who were present were staggered. To hear the truth not covertly, not alone with selected like-minded people, but

26

in a big auditorium, publicly, to share this happiness with others.
To hear the truth expressed in exact words.[39]

Galich's mounting reputation as a writer of underground songs, and probably this incident in particular, led to his being given a warning about his activites in May 1968 by the Secretariat of the Directorate of the Moscow Branch, Union of Writers, an incident for which the only documentary evidence is a passing reference in a Soviet source published ten years later, but which there is no reason to doubt.[40]

And then came the events of autumn 1968. That summer Galich spent in the small town of Dubna, south-west of Moscow and near the Tolstoi estate of Iasnaia Poliana; he was working on a screenplay about the life of the great bass Shaliapin for the prominent Soviet director Mark Donskov. He was joined there by Lev Kopelev and Raisa Orlova that August, and together they shared their reactions to the invasion of Czechoslovakia:

> Sasha and the two of us went into the forest. What would happen now? What would they do with us now? At that moment there was no doubt—it could only be mass terror. How else could it be, in what other way could they make the people swallow Prague?[41]

As we know, there was no mass terror; and seven brave individuals staged their demonstration on Red Square. The events of August 1968 form the subject of one of Galich's most anguished songs, *Petersburg Romance*. It is a summons to direct political action, and the anguish stems from the fact that the author himself is not prepared to take such action. But subsequent events were to drive him further and further towards this extreme.

At some time in 1968, a *samizdat* collection of Galich's songs, "published" in Moscow in 1967, penetrated to the West. It was reviewed in the NTS magazine *Posev;*[42] Galich was said to be someone who had returned from many years of prison and the camps. This review was reprinted as an afterword when the first book of Galich's songs, based on the *samizdat* text, was published in Frankfurt in 1969. This book contains forty-two songs, and constitutes the fundamental corpus of the songs that made Galich his original underground reputation.[43] Galich's refusal to disavow this book, which as a member of the Union of Writers he would have been expected to do, either voluntarily or with some prompting from the Union's minions, was one of the most serious charges against him when the Union eventually decided to call him to account.

The 1969 *Songs* is sufficient on its own to assure Galich a place among Russia's greatest satirists. It contains very little that has not stood the test of time, and most of the songs in it belong among the best that Galich ever was to write. Most of them kept a place in his concert repertoire until the end. In fact, the very last song in the book, *People Say There's Some Islands Somewhere,* was one of the last songs Galich ever sang in public, in Venice in December 1977. The one major element of Galich's work that is not reflected in *Songs* is of considerable importance, though, because it constitutes one of the most fundamental ways in which his work differs from that of his fellow poet-singers Okudzhava and Vysotsky. This is what might be called the "longer song" by analogy with the term "longer poem"; these longer songs, and the analogous grouping of shorter songs into thematically linked cycles, give Galich's work an epic dimension that is not found in the songs of the other poet-singers. There are three main longer works among Galich's songs. The first of them was published in 1971 anonymously, but with a tentative editorial attribution to Galich, under the title *Poem about Russia;*[44] its actual title, which became known later, is *Stalin*. The other longer songs are *Kaddish* and *Episodes from the Life of Klim Petrovich . . .;* they were first brought together in the collection which sums up the first stage of Galich's activity as a songwriter. This is the book called *Generation of the Accursed.*[45]

Besides the three longer works, this collection contains about one hundred shorter songs, and Galich was to add relatively little of substance to this corpus in the remaining years of his life. Among the shorter songs there is a small number of concise lyrical statements, like "In the Night There Comes . . . ," in which Galich makes a relatively straightforward autobiographical confession of position or mood. But the bulk of the songs are narrative ballads which in performance last five minutes or more. They are for the most part satirical genre pieces, "songs of everyday life" (*bytovye pesni*), which tell stories about specific characters in particular situations. The narration is sometimes impersonal, but in others the central characters themselves speak and tell their own stories.

The enormous range of characters created by Galich in these songs led the emigre literary scholar Efim Etkind to describe the songs as a "human comedy," a "model of our society," a small-scale but comparably wide-reaching parallel to Balzac's grandiose panorama of nineteenth-century French life.[46] The songs really do range over the whole of Soviet society; geographically from the most distant provinces to the offices of the highest servants of the state in the capital, and over the whole social gamut from peasants to professors; there are the victims and the victors of the Soviet historical experience, in their individual existences and in their co-existence. There is privilege and deprivation, favor and disfavor, health and sickness. And Galich gives these characters voices, an amazingly rich panoply of expression, intonation and register, often pinned down once and for all in a single pithy phrase.

The songs are deadly accurate in the way they capture the most striking and yet the most typical elements of Soviet social life—one task that official Socialist Realism is supposed to carry out, but manifestly does not. Galich goes far beyond merely mentioning the taboo subjects, such as the labor camps (*Clouds*); and he goes far beyond the standard and obvious subjects of complaint, like material shortages (*Guignol Farce*). He digs down into the stuff of the daily grind, the grim and exhausting struggle to carve out even a half-decent existence in the face of the monstrous dismalness of a bureaucratic, secretive, dogmatic, obscurantist, and at the same time pathologically self-congratulatory system. He does this with an epigrammatic sureness of touch, and an ever-open eye for the human pathos that the struggle continually points up.

Galich's language is always concentrated; a single phrase can conjure up whole vistas of connotation. This feature, of course, is central to the difficulties of translating Galich. One of his most perceptive critics, Natalia Rubenshtein, has pointed to several good examples in this connection. For example, the last stanza of *The Night Watch* begins with the line

The morning of our Motherland is pink.

To translate this literally presents no difficulty; but difficulty arises in connection with connotation. The line refers to a famous painting by F. Shurpin, *The Morning of Our Motherland*.[47] Natalia Rubenshtein relates that

In 1953, when Stalin died, I was in the seventh grade. Every year we used to write compositions based on the painting *The Morning of Our Motherland*. It used to hang in every school, every public bath, every savings bank ... Limitless fields. Electric pylons in the distance. A pink dawn just coming up. The Generalissimo in his grey tunic with his greatcoat over his arm. Russia's morning with the blessing of the Leader. If he hadn't been there, dawn would not have come up over the world, eternal gloom would have shrouded the endless expanses. "Man walks on, the master of his boundless Motherland" ... That's what just one line of Galich means to us![48]

Galich's songs are packed with references to Soviet institutions on all levels down to the most trivial details of everday life. They are perhaps the most culture-specific works of art that have been produced in post-war Russia. But their themes eventually raise issues that transcend this culture.

A substantial proportion of the genre songs deals with love affairs, which range in nature between the tragic, as in the story of the general's daughter, and the farcically sordid, as in the story of the "red triangle." Then there are the songs on Jewish themes, like *Warning;* the summit of this range is the long song *Kaddish,* with its implied parallel betwen the plight of the Polish Jews under Nazism and that of the Russian Jews in Galich's own time. In *Clouds* Galich created one of the classic statements about the GULAG experience. But besides writing about victims, Galich also wrote about the oppressors; *Stalin* is the summit of this particular theme. The "generation of the accursed" has its victors and its victims, but Galich is prepared to excuse neither side. In his *Goldminers' Waltz* he found one of the most laconic formulations yet made of the idea of silence as connivance:

> Many times, many ways we played silent parts,
> And our silence meant "yes" and not "no."

Galich's characters therefore share in a collective guilt. They are all involved in the crimes of their historical period. But they are not ennobled by their suffering, as is often the case with the "little men" of Russian literature; they are brutalized and made sordid.

And among this collective of guilty people Galich includes himself. In his first-person songs, he persistently expresses doubt as to his own fitness for the role of truth-teller. Underlying all the songs about modern Soviet life and the Stalin experience is Galich's own sense of personal guilt; he failed to act in the way he subsequently understood to be right, and he has not suffered. There is a constant note of self-reproach in Galich's work of the 1960s, a note that reaches its climax in the *Petersburg Romance* he wrote in August 1968—actually before the demonstration on Red Square about the Soviet invasion of Czechoslovakia.[49] Here, the anguished author, using the historical parallel of the ill-fated Decembrist rising of 1825 as the explicit subject, laments his failure to act in the face of an imperative need. But at the same time, Galich asserts that personal unworthiness does not invalidate the right of the individual to condemn what he sees to be wrong:

> It's the chosen alone who may judge?
> I'm not chosen, but I shall judge!

—as he says in one song (*Untitled*).

Galich's songs of the 1960s put before us a catalogue of disaster, failure, and guilt, in which there are no positive characters and nothing left of any ideals. The one note of consolation is an appeal to the effectiveness of dissent (however belated), and to the immortality of the poetic word. The ultimate statement of this faith is *We're no Worse than Horace*. This complex song, working on several planes at once in Galich's customary way, contrasts two kinds of dissent; on the one hand, there is seeming dissent which is part of the privileged, in-group life, "making V-signs in your pockets." But there are also genuine dissenters, whose activity is low-level and undemonstrative, but nevertheless effective, despite its miniscule scale:

> There's no hall, no red-plush auditorium,
> And no swooning claque to clap uproariously;
> Just an ordinary tape-recorder, but
> It's sufficient, there's no need for more than that.

It was this statement and others like it that made Galich a principal artistic spokesman for the heroic Soviet dissidents of the 1960s and his work the most concrete expression of their views.[50] The faith that motivated them all was that something actually could be achieved through resistance and truth-telling, however humble and insignificant the means might seem when compared with the mighty state apparatus against which they were ranged.

Set down on the page, divorced from Galich's own voice and accompaniment, the songs lose a great deal even in the original Russian. In his performances, Galich brought to bear the accumulated fruits of his long experience as actor and dramatist. He had an assured presence, a highly developed dramatic sense, and an absolute mastery of timing and delivery that gripped his audiences and enabled him to carry off effects that in the hands of a less accomplished talent would be cheap and vulgar. This personal charisma can be felt even from the tape recordings that were made in the 1960s. It is only in the author's performance that his poetry rises to its full stature. The guitar acts as the most rudimentary of props, furnishing a rhythmic springboard and underlining points of emphasis. Galich's voice, of un-remarkable tonal quality and sounding deliberately untrained, nevertheless possessed a remarkable range of expression, managing to encompass all the vast stylistic range of the poems—all the way from the stuttered expletives of the semi-literate worker to the high tradition of literary declamation, often within the compass of a single work. The melodies of the songs too are unremarkable, unlike the case with Okudzhava; they are usually not much more than loosely sketched lines over simple and repetitive harmonic patterns. However, effective use is made of contrasting melodies and tempi within the same song; only the very shortest songs use a single melody and metrical form throughout; and even then, the performance always brings in variations and contrasts. Galich's guitar technique is no more than adequate; he plucks single bass notes on the strong beats and fills in the bar with three- and four-note chords in the customary style of guitar-accompanied song in Russia; the guitar is never used on its own, except to provide rudimentary linking passages between stanzas and elementary introductions and codas.

Galich's choice of guitar-accompanied solo song was a deliberate decision arrived at for specific reasons.[51] As an experienced writer for films and stage, he was aware of and tuned in to the general shift in the dominant mode of perception away from the printed page towards the spoken word, and he decided that the "pre-Gutenberg" genre of the song would afford his message the maximum impact and penetration. His choice of sung poetry was made in the steps of Bulat Okudzhava, who had pioneered the revitalization of the genre, making his first public appearance in 1960.[52] As we know, though, Galich had been singing songs to his own guitar accompaniment since at least the early 1940s. As his access to an audience through official channels was progressively closed off from the late 1950s, he came to see song, now with the additional advantage of the domestic tape recorder as a medium for

31

preservation and transmission, as a way of obviating all the mechanisms of control and censorship that he had been contending with for so long in his career as a writer. The song offered immediacy: direct contact with the audience and instantaneous response. In a taped interview in 1974, he spelled these things out:

> I used to do plays and filmscripts, but I threw that business in completely in the early sixties; after all, poetry, and song even more, is the most suitable form for this machine standing here on the table. In this form it's easier to make an immediate response, to react straightaway, to do something impossible either in prose or the drama. I absolutely deliberately renounced my work in drama when I realized that it was only in this form that I could say everything I wanted, fully and to the end.[53]

Galich objected strongly to being called a "bard," the term that is common in Russian for the recent crop of poet-singers, and insisted that he was neither an entertainer nor a singer, as that word implied, but a Russian *poet,* who happened to have selected the genre of song as the most effective means available to him for communicating with the widest possible audience in a situation where the public media were strictly controlled and closed to him. The stylistic characteristics of his songs bear out this emphasis on the poetic word as a means of communication. Despite the packed allusiveness of the songs and their frequent use of grotesque juxtaposition of narrative planes, the songs do make an immediate impact:

> For me, poetry is always a cry for help, and I don't see the point when people start crying for help in incomprehensible language, because nobody will come to your help if you can't be understood.[54]

Accordingly, Galich's poetry steers clear of semantic complexity; its imagery is rarely recherche or self-consciously literary. It uses abundant phonetic patterning—inevitably lost in translation; and it uses repetition (in *Lenochka* and *The Mistake,* for example) to an extent that modern verse for reading shuns absolutely. The latter feature is the most obvious respect in which the songs lose when divorced from their music; the repetitions look merely repetitive, whereas in performance, usually with melodic variation and subtle changes of intonation, they can have very powerful and moving effects.

Another respect in which Galich's work loses in translation, and inevitably so, is that it is torn out of its original linguistic context, which is unique to the USSR in more ways than is customary for a national language. In a situation where the State-Party axis has a monopoly over the media, Galich, like all Russian writers (not only dissidents), felt that the language of public communication had been so debilitated as to become to a large extent meaningless:

> As you go around the city, you see these inscriptions on red bunting that mean absolutely nothing, written in "prefabricated," meaningless language. "PEOPLE AND PARTY ARE UNITED," "LET US MARK THE DECISIVE YEAR OF THE FIVE-YEAR PLAN" . . . Why are these signs hanging there, what information do they convey? Words are losing their meaning. And when you read a poem in a newspaper, you're driven to despair by this same absence of meaning. The word is a weapon which has been given us by the Lord, and which contains the essence and purpose of poetry . . .[55]

Galich's style in the songs was conceived as an antidote to this predicament. He brought into serious literary use a highly colloquial idiom completely purged of official and literary cliche (except for his murderous parodies of it); he mixed and juxtaposed linguistic registers in ways that are extremely bold when seen from the point of view of the conventions of Soviet literature and the wooden drabness of Soviet officialese.[56] But the startling freshness he achieved in his native language cannot be captured in translation; in other countries, the language of bureaucracy is not as all-pervading as in the USSR, and the language of literature is not as stultified and stereotyped; in fact, the language of literature has lost the ability to shock through the over-use of precisely those elements that Galich was among the first to bring in generous quantities into the language of serious literature in Russian.

Galich's desire for immediacy of impact through the use of song certainly had the effect that he wanted. His songs began to circulate widely and quickly in *magnitizdat* recordings; some of them rapidly "became folklore." Two examples of this may be cited. In 1969, the anti-Soviet journal *Grani,* in its regular feature called "From Our Correspondence with Russia" (whose inauthenticity there is no good reason to assume), published a letter from one "S. I." in Leningrad. It said that the most widespread literary genre was currently the political, criminal and humorous song. These are not underworld songs (*blatnye pesni*), but actually criminal songs (*ugolovnye pesni*) made up in the camps or by political prisoners.

> For example, there is a song called *Clouds* which is very popular now in the university; it was brought in from Kolyma. This is a song by a typical prisoner of Stalin's time, and it came in about two years ago . . .[57]

Perhaps more significant than this case is the fact that in his book about the USSR, written probably in 1968 and published outside the country in 1969, the then recently defected journalist Leonid Vladimirov, who had been close to the heart of Moscow literary life, retold the plot of Galich's *Ballad of Surplus Value,* mentioned its "enormous popularity," but was apparently unaware of the identity of the author.[58]

That official reprisals would be made against Galich was inevitable, given the content of his songs, even if he had made no attempt to publish them, and even if they had not been published outside the USSR with or without the author's consent or knowledge. His behavior had not been cautious; Raisa Orlova reports, for example, that Galich had sung *The Ballad of Surplus Value* in September 1967 from the platform of a packed auditorium in the Moscow House of Writers, the occasion being the sixtieth birthday celebrations for the short-story writer Nikolai Atarov. A member of the platform party on this occasion was Viktor Il'in, a general in the KGB and the highest-ranking security presence in the Union of Writers.[59] In November 1970, Galich along with Solzhenitsyn was elected a corresponding member of the most prominent dissident group, the Committee for Human Rights in the USSR, formed at that time by Academician Sakharov along with Tverdo-khlebov and Chalidze.[60] By 1971 there was ample evidence against Galich in the dossiers of the official watchdogs, and it was more or less a question of what incident would be used to bring him to book. It has been reported several times that the final straw came in late 1971 when Dmitry Poliansky, then Minister of Agriculture and a member of the Politburo, heard a tape of Galich's songs at his daughter's wedding reception and ordered an investigation.[61]

Eventually, on 29 December 1971, Galich was expelled from the Union of Writers; his expulsion from the Union of Cinematographers followed shortly thereafter. He was charged with not disavowing the publication of his work abroad, and encouraging Soviet Jews to emigrate to Israel, "crimes incompatible with the high calling of Soviet writer."[62] The most striking indication of the seriousness with which Galich's work was viewed in official circles was that he was expelled not only from the Union of Writers, but simultaneously from the Litfond, the body which controls and administers financial aid to writers;[63] the only known precedent for this step had been the case of Solzhenitsyn. These measures meant that not only would theaters and publishing houses withdraw and in future boycott Galich's work, but that he would not in the future be able to collect royalties or receive support payments. He was, in fact, made into a literary unperson.

One incident in the expulsion proceedings was specially painful for Galich. It involved the dramatist Alexei Arbuzov, one of the leaders of the collective as part of which Galich had helped to write *City of the Dawn* back in 1940. In 1957, Arbuzov published this play under his own name. Galich's scornful denunciation of this act evidently got back to Arbuzov, and there was an element of personal score-settling when he denounced Galich at the meeting in December 1971:

At the meeting when they expelled me, Arbuzov got his own back, . . . calling me a "marauder." As proof he cited the lines from *Clouds:*

> Once I froze like iron to ice,
> Digging roads with pick in hand;
> Not for nothing I blew away
> Twenty years in those labor camps!

"But I've known Galich since 1940!" exclaimed Arbuzov with pathos. "I know for a fact that he's never done time!" . . . And then, in a voice full of pain and bitterness, Arbuzov said some more heartfelt words about how shaken he was by the depths to which I had sunk, and how he'd been unable to sleep as he prepared for today's tribunal. He was so convincingly regretful that everyone who spoke after him seemed to forget what they had come together for, and they talked not so much about me and my transgressions as about how they had been shaken and disturbed by Arbuzov's speech, how they sympathized with him and would try to help.[64]

Galich was now excluded from the world of official Soviet literature, a world he had inhabited for practically forty years.

He spent the summer of 1972 in the village of Zhukovka, where Academician Sakharov, Alexander Solzhenitsyn, and Mstislav Rostropovich were also living. Raisa Orlova, who was also there with her husband Lev Kopelev, relates that Galich was deeply offended by Solzhenitsyn's refusal to see him, especially in view of their common recent experience of expulsion from the Union of Writers and the Litfond. At this same time he became good friends with Sakharov, whose second wife, Elena Bonner, he had known since the days before the war when they had both been involved with the Pluchek-Arbuzov theater.[65] It was during this summer that Galich openly became part of the dissident movement by signing two collective open letters written by Sakharov, one about capital punishment and the other a call for an amnesty for political prisoners. He was to continue signing; on 22 March 1973 he signed another joint open letter to UNESCO pointing out the dangers of increased censorship of individual authors as a result of the recent signing by the USSR of the International Copyright Convention. Then, together with Sakharov and Vladimir Maximov he wrote to the government of Chile in defense of Pablo Neruda; this was on 18 September 1973. In the same month he supported Sakharov's candidature for a Nobel Peace Prize. On 5 January 1974, together with Sakharov, Maximov, Voinovich and Shafarevich he signed an open letter in defense of Solzhenitsyn. Two other letters in defense of persecuted writers followed; in favor of Bukovsky to the League in Defence of Human Rights, on 27 February 1964; and on 18 March on behalf of the imprisoned literary scholar Gabriel Superfin.[66]

It was probably at some time in 1972 that Galich was received into the Orthodox Church. There is no evidence of a movement towards this decision in Galich's artistic work before this date. His conversion seems paradoxical to many people. Raisa Orlova comments:

> ... As an unbeliever it is not given to me to make judgments about this. The only thing I can say is that after putting on the cross, Galich (like certain other new converts) became no better and no more merciful, nor did he start thinking about other people. But this has to do with his personality, not his artistic creative work.[67]

In addition, his health was giving increasing cause for concern. He had been in and out of the hospital with a chronic heart condition since the mid-forties. In the spring of 1971 he had been within a hair's-breadth of death after picking up an infection from a syringe that a Leningrad doctor used when summoned to deal with a heart attack.[68] This incident is related in the major work that Galich completed during his time as an unperson, the autobiographical *The Dress Rehearsal.* This book was written in and around Moscow in 1973 and published abroad in the following year. In it, Galich sometimes makes forays back into his earliest childhood memories; these and later incidents are woven into the central incident in the book, the story of the doomed dress rehearsal of Galich's play, *Sailor's Rest;* the complete script of the play is included in the book. It contains some of the most interesting discussion yet published of the internal workings of the control system in Soviet literature, and it deserves to be better known both on account of this and for the testament it contains of Galich's personal evolution from accepted Soviet writer to outcast unperson. The book is a closing of the account, an attempt to take stock of the author's life up to the point of writing, when he was in his mid-fifties.

During this increasingly difficult time, Galich continued to give recitals of his songs. Several eye-witness accounts of these performances have been published. Vladimir Naumov met Galich in 1971:

> Galich sang at our house several times. His performances always happen as follows. In a friend's flat the invited people gather; drinks and sandwiches appear on the table; tape recorders are switched on; and about 10 to 15 people, sometimes more, fall under the spell of "the famous Galich" who sings "underground songs." As he sings, he experiences everything afresh. Sometimes he finds it painful to sing, sometimes he can't help laughing. Before every song he says a few words, explains things that are obscure or tells the story of how the song came about.[69]

Galich would receive people in his Moscow flat and allow them to record his songs, refusing any fee; however, some would surreptitiously leave money, knowing the man's circumstances. To help him get together the money for his departure when he eventually decided to go, he was invited to Leningrad, where he made a six-hour recording of all his songs in chronological order with detailed commentary; for this he received as a fee the utmost that the organizers could get from his admirers.[70]

But it was clear from the moment of his expulsion from the unions that the authorities meant to get rid of him; and his plight was actually hopeless. In January 1974, he applied for and was refused permission to leave the country. Sakharov, with his wife and Vladimir Maximov, wrote an open letter about his predicament to the International PEN Club and the European Association of Writers:

> In our country there are few people unfamiliar with Galich's songs ... Two years ago the secretariat of the writers' union, obligingly obeying the order of its ideological bosses, expelled Galich from membership in the union. It was an act of reprisal for his free-thinking and popularity. For two years this valiant man, who is suffering from a serious heart ailment, has withstood almost unbearable living conditions, literally struggling for his day-to-day existence. Only when he was faced with complete poverty did he apply for permission to visit relatives in the U. S. for a rest cure. On January 14 Alexander Galich was called to the Moscow visa department and told in the presence of some man in civilian clothes that he could not make the trip for "ideological reasons."[71]

It was clear that Galich was not going to be allowed the fiction of a temporary visa which would enable him to leave the country as a Soviet citizen—even if he were to be stripped of his citizenship as soon as he got abroad. On 3 February 1974, Galich felt compelled to write to the International Commission for Human Rights. He complained about being refused permission to leave the country, and then described his current situation in the following words:

> In the two and more years that have passed since my expulsion from the Union of Writers and the Union of Cinematographers, I have been deprived of other, professional, rights: the right to see my work published, the right to enter into contracts with theaters, film studios, and publishing houses, the right to make public pronouncements. When films for which I in the past have written the screenplay are shown now, some hidden hand excises my name from the credits. I am not just an

untouchable, but an unmentionable too. The only time my name is mentioned, and then to the accompaniment of insulting and abusive epithets, is occasionally at various closed meetings, to which I am denied entry. The only right I still have is the right to reconcile myself to my total lack of rights, to acknowledge that at 54 my life is essentially over, to collect my invalid's pension of 60 roubles a month, and to shut up. And wait.

Anything at all can happen to a person in my position. In view of the extreme danger of this position I am compelled to turn for help to you, the International Commission for Human Rights, and through you to writers, musicians, people of the theater and cinema, to all those who, probably out of naivete, continue to believe that a person has the right to freedom of word and conscience, the right to leave his country at will and return to it.[72]

In the final paragraph of this letter Galich linked his predicament with that of Vladimir Maximov, who had also just been refused permission to go abroad.

The decision to try and leave Russia must have been a particularly bitter one for Galich. After all, he had written the defiant *Song of Exodus* (dated 20 December 1971), wishing his departing friends well, but insisting that he was not going to leave:

I will remain on this soil.
Someone, after all, despite his fatigue,
Must stand guard on the peace of our dead!

The inexorable deterioration of his position after he was deprived of the ability to earn his living, though, made Galich eat his words. He told Raisa Orlova:

I wrote *Song of Exodus* a year ago, and I sincerely believed that I would stay. But now I've decided to go . . . it's all very difficult. I've got no prospects here. I couldn't stand any more summonses to the procurator's office. My life isn't over yet. I want to see something of the world. I want to hold my book in my hands . . . [73]

Eventually, in June 1974, Galich was given twenty-four hours to get out of the country; and he left, as it turned out, never to return.

Thus, Galich's turn to songwriting and "guitar poetry" in 1962 led him in the course of a dozen years to lose everything he had acquired in his years as a Soviet writer: status, money, possessions, an assured and comfortable future. He had now lost his native country with its precious linguistic environment. His health was damaged. When he applied to leave the USSR, he had nothing left to lose; he was unpersoned and had no possibility whatsoever of making a come-back into literature in the foreseeable future. It was becoming ever more clear that the authorities were not satisfied with silencing him and depriving him of his livelihood; they wanted him either dead or out of the country.

In 1973, when he was staying at the country club for the actors of the Bolshoi Theater in Serebrianyi Bor, a riverside resort in the western suburbs of Moscow, Galich noticed a peculiar mechanism standing by the entrance to the grounds. Over a wooden column, marked off into numbered divisions, ran a string; at one end was a weight that gave a reading on the numbers; the other end of the string disappeared into the ground. The caretaker explained to Galich that the thing stood over the cess-pit. The invisible end of the string was attached to a float on the surface of the pit's contents, and as the level rose, so the weight at the end of the string showed a higher reading on the column. The groundsman called the mechanism a "shitometer" (*govnomer*); and in it, Galich saw an image that symbolized his own position as a satirist in Soviet society—and also gave us one of the most striking definitions of the historical function of the Russian writer.

> All was grey and clouded over,
> The woods standing as if dead;
> Just the weight of the shitometer
> Very gently nods its head.
> In this world not all's in vain
> (Though it mayn't be worth two bits!)
> Just so long as there are weights
> So you can *see* the level of the shit.

The Wild West

Galich had psychologically prepared himself for emigration in a way that apparently has no parallel among the recent crop of political deportees from the USSR. In a way that he later compared to a mother taking her child into a house where there was measles so it should be infected and get over the disease once and for all, he attempted to inoculate himself against nostalgia before actually leaving his country, by writing a cycle of poems in which he imagined separation from his favorite places while still actually being in them (*An Attempt at Nostalgia,* or perhaps *An Essay in Nostalgia*).

He left Russia in mid-June 1974 by the normal route for Jewish emigres, by air from Moscow to Vienna. After a brief stop in Frankfurt, though, he left for Oslo. Through the artist Victor Sparre he had connections in Norway, among other things an invitation from the Scandinavian Society of New Converts to Christianity. For the first year of his emigration he was based in Norway, giving lectures in the University of Oslo on the history of the Russian theater. He explained his choice of this culturally remote city by saying that his experiences of the last few years, and especially his deteriorating health, made him want to rest rather than plunging straight into emigre literary and political affairs, and also that he felt a sense of obligation to Norway for the invitation and for the hospitality he had been shown on his previous visit as a Soviet writer.

However much he may have complained of fatigue, though, he was never idle. Several projects were got under way without delay: a translation into Norwegian of *The Dress Rehearsal,* eventually published by the major firm Guldenal in 1975; and the first recording Galich made under professional studio conditions. This was an album made at Arne Bendiksen Studios, released in 1975 under the title *A Whispered Cry.*

Besides these things, he undertook a strenuous program of concert appearances. He appeared in Geneva on 9 September, then in Berne, Zurich, and Brussels, where on 15 September he gave a concert for the Russian emigre organization and received a warm reception from a packed house. In its notice of the concert, the newspaper *Russkaia mysl',* which takes a dim view of all things Soviet—including in this category most of the things undertaken by the second and third emigrations from the USSR—somewhat surprisingly observed that Galich was

> the model of an old Russian member of the intelligentsia, completely untouched by the Soviet disease, possessing substantial culture, remarkable kindness and politeness, a sensitive attitude towards people and nobility of spirit.[74]

There followed another triumph in Paris, at this time the capital of the Russian emigrations; from there Galich went to London, where he sang to a packed house at the Commonwealth Institute on 5 November. After this he performed in Munich, where he was to move about after a year in Oslo.

The reason for the move to Munich was to take up a post with Radio Liberty, the American-sponsored station that broadcasts to Eastern Europe and the USSR. Galich started making regular broadcasts in the autumn of 1974, under the title "Alexander Galich Speaks and Sings"; his programs were mainly recitals of his own songs, supplied with commentaries explaining their origin and ideas. Galich worked from Munich until in late 1976 he became Director of the cultural section of Radio Liberty in Paris. The move to Paris brought him into close proximity with another enterprise with which he had been associated since he left Russia; this was the journal *Kontinent,* the most forceful and prosperous organ of the "third emigration." It had been founded in 1974 by Vladimir Maximov, and Galich had been a member of its international advisory board from the very beginning. It was on the pages of *Kontinent* that most of the work written after his emigration was published.

Perhaps the most demanding undertaking Galich performed in emigration was to make concert tours in Israel. As a person of Jewish origin who had been a spokesman, through his songs, for the "new exodus" of Jews from the USSR that got under way in the early 1970s, but who had then converted to Orthodox Christianity and emigrated not to Israel, as he was strictly speaking required to do, but to Europe, Galich was an enigmatic personality, to say the least, from the point of view of right-thinking Israelis. He made two tours to Israel, in November 1975 and the autumn of 1976. The first tour, during which he gave fifteen concerts in three weeks, was an overwhelming success, with packed halls, and wide coverage in the press and on TV. Galich related that he had

> ... never seen such enormous concert halls. In Tel Aviv, for example, it was a 2800-seater. I gave two shows one after the other and all the seats were sold. It was the same in Jerusalem, in the Teatron, where the 2000-seater hall was too small and a lot of people had to sit on the steps, behind the curtains, and on the stage. It was the same in Haifa.[75]

The second tour, in 1976, was much less successful, with audiences of below one thousand in the places that earlier had been packed.[76]

The next year, 1977, was especially busy for Galich. In April he finished putting together a new book of poems, which bore the title *When I Return ...*, echoing the not-daring-to-hope mood of its keynote piece. This book contains the full version of the Klim Petrovich cycle, now swelled to six items. But of the total of six sections contained in the book, only one concerns Galich's new environment, the west; *The Wild West*, as he calls it. The west is not wild with the savagery of the cowboy;

> There's a different game going on here;
> On purpose, they drink Polish vodka
> With Moscow caviare.
>
> Here in the West that's been sold out
> And crucified for the sake of a bet,
> In their Parises and Londons,
> The savage natives live like devils!
>
> Bewitched by the beginnings
> Of unheard-of speeds,
> Stupified by their Sartres
> Of all sizes and breeds!

The cycle expresses that enraged frustration with the liberalism of the west, its tolerance towards the ideologies of eastern Europe, that has become more and more widespread among Russians of the third emigration, and especially

41

among the intellectuals associated with *Kontinent,* whose editor, Vladimir Maximov, has expressed this attitude with the greatest force in his *Saga of the Rhinos.*

Galich was variously reported to be working now on prose, either a short story or a novel. He did in fact complete the first part of a novel called *The Flea Market,* whose action is set in Odessa among the criminal element and its associates.[77] He also said that he wanted to write

> another thing like *The Dress Rehearsal,* from life, but without the inserts. After all, I wanted to publish *Sailor's Rest,* but plays don't sell well, though if I reworked it, it would sell.[78]

In the same interview he spoke about a book whose idea would be to counter the Soviet image of the NTS, the anti-Soviet emigre organization with which Galich had become closely associated. Late in 1977 he began a new series of broadcasts for Radio Liberty, with a very pronounced satirical tone, called "Galich in Paris reads the Soviet newspapers." During the course of 1977 he was in Italy no less than seven times; the penultimate occasion was to participate in the "Sakharov Hearings" in Rome; and then in December he took part in the Venice Biennale, which was devoted to the discussion and exposition of dissident art from Eastern Europe. It was during the Biennale, on 3 December, that he gave his very last concert.

Galich had anticipated this almost frantic level of activity in the first interview he gave after he left Russia. He was asked if he would survive as a poet outside his native linguistic environment; he agreed that things might be more difficult, but that

> I'm not a boy, I'm a person who's lived. In the course of these years I've accumulated and worked up so much that I hope God will grant me the time to finish, here in the west, everything I started or intended to write in the Soviet Union.[79]

In the same interview he said that he had not gone to Israel because as a poet he would not have wanted to follow the state's policy and assimilate, thus losing his native Russian. And finally, he identified his general standpoint with the one expressed in Solzhenitsyn's celebrated pamphlet calling on his fellow Russians not to live the lie; he condemned

> lies, injustice, the fact that the splendid slogans about "freedom, equality and fraternity" disguise an essentially undisguised state of arbitrary rule, violence, spiritual enslavement, moral deafness and blindness that exists at the present time in Soviet Russia.[80]

42

Galich continued to emphasize the contribution he felt he had to make. The very last interview he gave to the emigre press appeared late in November 1977. In it, he spoke emphatically about the need for the three waves of Russian emigres to come together and put behind them the internecine squabbling that was exactly what their common enemy most desired. On the subject of emigration, he used a phrase that has become something of a commonplace; this was that the Russian emigres are "not sent away, but sent forth" (*ne v izgnanii, a v poslanii*), an idea first formulated by one of the most outstanding figures of the first emigration, the poet and critic Zinaida Gippius (1869-1945). Galich commented:

> ... at first I thought that being "sent forth" was too weighty a phrase, but later, gradually, I became convinced that it's right. Russia, the spirit of the Russian people, has so to speak sent us forth into other countries, with a single purpose—to preserve our spiritual culture, to take it into the world, to nurture it, and if we have the strength, to increase it.[81]

The essentially passive concept of conservation that is primary in this idea of being "sent forth" as guardians of Russia's cultural heritage, though, was not something that Galich would accept. All through the emigre period of his life, he was concerned with the problem of breaking through the language barrier and reaching an audience wider than his faithful Russian devotees. Galich had more on his side than do most emigre writers; his preferred medium, song, involved music as well as words; and he possessed consummate skill and experience in putting over his work to live audiences. But it was quite clear to those who saw him work in front of a foreign audience that the cumbersome process of the reading of a translation in whatever language was required, perhaps even with explanatory observations about the *realia* involved in the words, before the author himself performed the original, could not but destroy that gripping immediacy that Galich's appearances had for his compatriots. Galich himself remained optimistic, but under no illusions:

> My appearances in Italy have convinced me that with a good interpreter it is possible to appear in front of an audience that doesn't understand Russian. There's nothing you can compare with the joy you feel when you're in contact with Russians, though. It was like that in Ostia in front of new emigres who were waiting to leave for various different countries, and it was like that in Milan, where there was a hall full of Russians. Consequently I long very much for my Russian audience.[82]

The most paradoxical thing about Galich's situation as an emigre was precisely to do with contact with his audience at home. Through his work on radio, he undoubtedly reached a bigger audience in Russia from outside the country than he had while he remained unpersoned and persecuted inside it; and what is more, unlike those writers whose work reached its authentic audience through the artificial mediation of the air-waves instead of as words printed on the page and intended for silent private reading, Galich's work came as it was meant to be—in the author's own performance, aurally perceived, with his own accompaniment. And, of course, it was taped by the Russian audience from his broadcasts and circulated and transmitted in the way it had since the early 1960s—through *magnitizdat*.

The most eloquent tribute to Galich's continuing presence as a force to be reckoned with inside the USSR even after he had been physically hounded out of it was the attention he began to get in the Soviet media. After years of total silence while he was still in Moscow—there was never any public discussion of his songs, unlike the case with Okudzhava and even Vysotsky—Galich now started to come in for some vicious abuse. As an employee of Radio Liberty he was regularly mentioned in the routine smear stories about this organization with which the Soviet authorities aim to discredit it with the Soviet public (which listens to it avidly). The customary line is that Radio Liberty is a catspaw organization of the CIA manned by a gang of renegade Russian traitors and common criminals who dance to the tune of their American controllers. For example, in January 1976 *Pravda* asserted:

> Because time takes its toll, Liberty is being forced to fill up its vacancies at the moment. Among the novices are some people who have used emigration to Israel as a pretext but who in fact never intended to go there. Once they got over the Soviet frontier, they immediately surfaced in the camp of the enemies of the Soviet system. In the last analysis there's no bad without good, for their work for Radio Liberty has helped Galich, Belotserkovskii and others demonstrate their anti-Soviet instincts to the full.[83]

Galich's name was dragged by *Literaturnaia gazeta* into its scurrilous account of the suicide of a recent emigre, Elena Stroeva, in May 1976.[84] Four Soviet journalists working for *Izvestiia* put together a denunciation of the third emigration which was first published under the title *Caught Red-Handed* in 1976. Here, Galich is said to have "abandoned two wives and daughters one after the other" and to be "a hopeless drunkard, who emigrated to Israel after being accepted into the Orthodox Church," but to have settled in Europe, where "he has remained a carouser and has got into debt."[85] The second edition of this book, now with the title *Absolutely Secret,* published the year after the first edition, goes rather further:

> This "Russian bard" who has recorded beerhall anti-Soviet songs, has managed to settle two wives in his flat at one time, and is

awaiting the arrival of a third. There's only one thing that gets him down—he's drunk away his earnings for six months in advance and because of this, the representatives of the institution concerned have not only put a lien on his salary but also had an appraisal of all his property carried out.[86]

And so the persecution of Galich continued, even after he had had to leave the country.

Galich died on Thursday 15 December 1977 as a result of an accident at home. He came back to his flat and without even taking off his overcoat went to plug in his new tape recorder (radio receiver, according to some accounts); there was a short circuit, and he was electrocuted. His wife was out at the time. A funeral service was held on 22 December at the Russian church on the rue Daru, and Galich was buried in the Russian cemetery at Ste Geneviève-des-Bois.

The announcement of Galich's death in *Le Monde* on 17 December 1977 stated that his body had been taken to the Institute of Forensic Medicine for an autopsy by two experts, Bailly and Martin, and also that the police had ordered an examination of the equipment that had killed Galich. The findings of the police autopsy were made public on 20 December, and the cause of death was stated to be electrocution after touching a bare wire, "apparently while trying to repair a tape recorder." The death was pronounced accidental.[87]

Another report of Galich's death said that it was his radio he had intended to turn on, but that he plugged the aerial into the wrong socket and received an electric shock.[88] And a Radio Liberty broadcast by one of his former colleagues recounted the last official activity of his life:

On 15 December Alexander Galich came in early to the Paris correspondents' office of Radio Liberty, where he had been working for a year. He looked tired. He had just got back from Venice, and had fallen ill on his way back to Paris. He came in for the morning conference of the Radio Liberty correspondents, exchanged a few words with us, said he didn't feel well and was going home for a rest, and then a few hours later we received the terrible news of his death.[89]

The last book Galich prepared for the press, *When I Return,* was published only about a week after his death. The Afterword has inevitably given rise to speculation that Galich knew what was going to happen; he cites Eisenstein's dictum that the film-maker should shoot every single frame as if it were the last he would ever make and applied this to his own work as a poet:

Every single poem, every line, and even more every book, is the last one.

45

It follows that this is my last book.
Although at the bottom of my heart I hope, all the same, that
I'll manage to write something more.[90]

In the overheated atmosphere of emigre life, Galich's death is still the subject for speculation and rumor. The rumors have been fed by the Soviet media, which continue to harrass even Galich's shade. On 17 April 1978, the weekly supplement to *Izvestiia* published an article painting the blackest possible picture of Galich's life after he left Russia. It alleged that he had led a completely debauched life, that he had abandoned his wife, experienced constant friction with Radio Liberty's American masters, proved an incompetent administrator, got himself deeply into debt, and so on and so on. The contradictions in the accounts of Galich's death, asserted this article, left ample room to speculate that the CIA had eventually found Galich more trouble than he was worth to them and "arranged" his death by supplying him with faulty radio equipment.[91] The inevitable counter-blast to this report came from Mikhail Agursky, who asserted that its real aim was to suggest to the Soviet reader that it was actually the long arm of the KGB that had caused Galich's death.[92]

It seems unavoidable that a figure as imposing as Galich will continue to generate legends even after his death, just as during his life it was generally assumed that his songs must be autobiographical and the author a living legend.

Fame is the Spur

Alexander Galich was one of a large number of Russian writers this century who have made the decision to renounce success, actual or potential, for the sake of their own vision of the truth. To start with, there were all the writers who emigrated after the revolution, braving a future probably without a reading public—though many of them thought at the time that their work would be allowed back into Russia if the Soviet state managed to establish itself. Then there were those who remained in Russia and sooner or later chose silence, like Sologub, Akhmatova, and others. More relevant for the Soviet writers who were formed in the post-revolutionary environment was the example of Evgeny Zamiatin, the first actual Communist writer to renounce his allegiance to the Soviet state and ask to emigrate, which permission he received in 1932 after petitioning Stalin in a famous letter of 1931. And the dramatist and novelist Mikhail Bulgakov (1891-1940), with whose work Galich's songs have often been compared because of their element of the grotesque, continued to write fiction that he knew could never be published in the USSR. Osip Mandelstam and Evgenii Shvarts persisted in writing their own unorthodox work during the worst years of Stalinism. And there were others. But the immediate and real precedent for Galich's actions, as for so many other modern Russian writers, was that of Boris Pasternak, whose stature by the late 1950s as the leading living Russian poet was undubitable. Perhaps without any degree of calculating forethought, Pasternak accepted the disastrous practical consequences for his career and prospects that the publication of his novel *Doctor Zhivago* abroad would probably entail after it had been turned down for publication in the USSR. This happened in 1957, and it was the current talking-point among Soviet writers at the time when Galich was experiencing his first serious *contretemps* with the literary authorities.

After Pasternak, established Soviet writers have been renouncing their allegiance in what seems to be an endless stream. The most senior of them was Alexander Bek (1903-1972); he had been publishing prose since 1934, and had produced a classic Soviet war novel, *The Volokolamsk Highway,* in 1944-45. But he spent the last ten years of his life at work on a novel which had no hope of publication in the USSR, *The New Appointment.* Published abroad in 1972, this novel contains the most convincing portrayal of Stalin that has yet appeared. After Bek came Vasily Grossman (1905-1964), who became a top-flight Soviet writer with the publication of his war novel *The People is Immortal* (1942). After the banning and the grotesque confiscation of the second part of the novel *For a Just Cause,* he dedicated himself to the completion of a novel that could not possibly have been published in the USSR; it circulated in *samizdat* since 1963 and was published abroad under the title *Forever Flowing* in 1970. Bek and Grossman, renouncers of the 1960s, remained in the USSR as underground writers. Their successors, with a few exceptions such as Georgy Vladimov, have had to leave the country. Anatoly Kuznetsov, who defected from a group of Soviet writers in London in 1969, was a transitional figure; Kuznetsov (1929-1979) was the author of a classic Soviet novel, *Babii Iar* (1966).

After Kuznetsov came the decade of expulsions, of which Galich's was one. Perhaps the closest renouncer to Galich in terms of literary approach, if not in seniority as a Soviet writer, is Andrei Siniavsky (b. 1925), who was just beginning to make a big name for himself as an academic literary critic when in 1956, inspired by the atmosphere in the wake of Khrushchev's "Secret Speech" he wrote the essay *What is Socialist Realism?,* which remains one of the most penetrating exposes of the official "artistic method" of Soviet literature and the arts in general; and then, using the pseudonym "Abram Tertz," Siniavsky began writing short stories that make liberal use of grotesque fantasy, like some of Galich's songs. The earliest of them, *The Trial Begins,* was deliberately sent for publication in France late in 1956, actually before the "Zhivago affair"; it was followed by a stream of other stories that eventually led to Siniavsky's arrest along with his friend Iuly Daniel in October 1965, and their trial the next year. This trial was a watershed in the history of Soviet literary dissent. After serving his time, Siniavsky preceded

Galich into emigration by one year. The next forced emigration was so momentous that it has overshadowed all the others—that of Solzhenitsyn in February 1974. Four months before Galich, Vladimir Maximov arrived in Paris. Born in 1932, Maximov had been regarded as a well-established Soviet novelist and editor; his refusal to continue compromising with the texts of his works had eventually brought him to the point of no return. In September 1974, three months after Galich, Viktor Nekrasov left the USSR. Eight years older than Galich, Viktor Nekrasov is the most senior Soviet writer among the exiles of the 1970s. He had emerged in 1946 with the Stalin Prize-winning novel known in English as *Front-Line Stalingrad,* based on his own experience as a fighting infantry officer, and by the early 1960s was a trusted Soviet writer, a member of the Communist Party and a pillar of the literary establishment. Because of his writings during the 1960s Nekrasov came to be more and more at odds with the literary authorities; eventually, in 1969, he was expelled from the Party, and in 1972 decreed an unperson, shortly after this same indignity had been visited upon Galich.

The first decade of expulsions culminated in 1980 with the departures of Vladimir Voinovich, Vasily Aksenov, and Lev Kopelev with his wife Raisa Orlova (the two close friends of Galich whose words have been frequently cited earlier). Aksenov has given a graphic account of the accumulating frustration that eventually brought matters to a head for him, one of the most vaunted of the youthful writers whose work had once seemed to promise a renaissance of Soviet literature in the 1960s.[94] And it should not be forgotten that all these renouncers, writers who had made themselves a name in Soviet literature, have been accompanied into exile by dozens of authors—led by Joseph Brodsky in 1972—who had either been refused entry into Soviet literature or had disdained to seek it.

There is no universal, simple explanation for the actions of this—by now very large—number of renouncers. Each one had his own motives, each followed his own complex path towards the eventual renunciation. There have been the most widely differing theories advanced in explanation of Galich's actions; some of them were mentioned earlier. They range from the blunt phrase used by Galich himself to Iury Krotkov: "I was sick of serving," to Vladimir Maximov's high-flown words in his obituary of his friend:

> In Galich there existed in truth Chekhov's ideal of human beauty: "Soul, face, and dress." His deeply rooted and strikingly natural artistry made itself felt in everything—his daily life, his creative work, his dealings with people. Any disharmony, whether it concerned ethics or aesthetics, caused him torments of suffering. It seems to me that it was just this quality of soul and character that eventually led this pure actor, poet and singer into the ranks of our democratic movement.[95]

The most obvious paradoxes about Galich were pointed out in a brash review of one of his concerts during the first tour of Israel by a student called R. Danielson. He admitted that such songs as the Klim Petrovich cycle, *Clouds, Ballad of Surplus Value,* and *The Red Triangle* were masterpieces, but took strong exception both to Galich's overtly Christian songs and also to *Kaddish,* taking the latter to be a gross breach of taste. However, Danielson continued:

> From Ginzburg he became Galich.
> The "convict-singer," he was never in a camp.
> The "warrior-singer," he was never at the front.
> He wrote "You leave, but I will stay," and then left ... for Norway.
> Apparently a Jew ("See my sabbath star burn"), he was converted to apparent Orthodoxy.[96]

But the main point of Danielson's argument was that these contradictions were only seeming ones, and that the essence of Galich was "an amazing realization of Stanislavsky's system, where the actor lives his part"; and "it's an actor's way to change parts. He can't be reproached for that."

There is clearly little point in pursuing the question of Galich's essential sincerity; there is equally little point in disputing the reality of the self-sacrifice his actions entailed. We can never know what would have happened to Galich if he had been spared the "guignol farce" that cut short his life. But he was a unique figure, even when seen against the background of the catalogue of renunciations by his contemporaries and younger fellows among Soviet writers. He was unique because so far he has been the only case of what might be called an "average" Soviet writer turning against his situation. During his career as dramatist and scenarist, Galich wrote nothing of any lasting artistic value, nothing even that was regarded by orthodox Soviet criticism as having outstanding merit. But when he started writing satirical songs, he produced work of great and lasting importance. He took a genre that was coming into vogue through the work of Okudzhava and some others, and transformed it into a vehicle for devastating social comment and political satire. Using language and images, characters and situations that were highly culture-specific, he nevertheless in his best works transcended these limitations and spoke of the human condition in general. In the space of less than a decade, some of Galich's songs won the greatest honor that poetry can receive: their author's identity was forgotten and they "became folklore." This was a monumental achievement; not only were the songs denied access to any means of legitimate publication and circulation, but the entire ethos of the ruling culture was ranged against them with its massive apparatus and economic monopoly. Galich's songs penetrated to and were accepted by the people because he gave them a credible interpretation of their authentic experience; and with a power and concision matched by no other post-war

Russian satirist, Galich exposed the sham of the official presentation of that experience.

But even granted the sensitivity of Galich's ear for spoken language and his ability to define a character in a few well-chosen strokes, the fruit of his years as a professional dramatist, it was not these skills that made his work unique. What powered Galich's songs of the 1960s was the individual psyche of the author, and above all else it was his conscience. This was the guilty conscience, allied with a powerful dose of self-contempt, of a man who for years had served the system as a Soviet writer. The songs were in expiation of this guilt. Galich sang about those who had actually suffered from the moral position of one who had not. Despite his conviction concerning the universality of guilt, this position caused Galich real anguish.

Galich's anguish is a phenomenon apparently without parallel among dissident Russian writers. It lies at the opposite extreme of the spectrum from the cynicism of Shostakovich. Galich was not a believer in "inner freedom" (or "secret freedom"), where the essential intangibility of the creative spirit eventually vitiates the actual interference with the end-products of that process by forces that are not part of it. Neither was he a dissembler by nature. His character was perhaps essentially that of an actor, but he certainly suffered when he was playing more than one role at once. In the 1960s, up to the time Galich was brought to book by the Soviet authorities, he was living a double life, and his awareness of this was the driving force of his satirical vision. After 1971, when he was outlawed, he was no longer living a double life, and he had become numbered among those who had truly suffered. His acceptance into the Orthodox Church was a further step towards spiritual peace and reconciliation.

But the move away from a double life, on the one hand writing and performing underground songs, and on the other continuing to be a member of the Union of Writers, the Union of Cinematographers, and the Litfond, seems to have cost Galich's creative talent dear. For when Galich turned away from satire, as he did in many of the songs in *When I Return ...*, moved away from dramatic confrontation to confession,[97] and tried to turn satire against something other than the system he grew up with (as in *The Wild West*), he lost his vital spark. Where the songs of the 1960s are particular, concrete, full of maximally concentrated images that evoke an entire society, the non-satirical work is flaccid, vague, and even sentimental.

Galich's creative life was not a smooth progression from one stage to another. He switched fairly abruptly out of orthodoxy into dissidence, and in doing so switched genres, from solemn plays to satirical songs. Forgettable as a Soviet writer, he became immortal as a Russian satirist. When he became an emigre, first internal and then external, he wrote fewer and fewer songs, more and more spoken poems, and then prose fiction and memoirs. Paradoxically, as an emigre he was able to reach his audience more effectively than he had when he was still in Russia and unable to generate or control broadcasts of his work over the radio. But his real contribution belonged to the past; and when he left Russia, becoming a writer whose outcast status was consistent with his dissident attitudes, the resulting spiritual peace and clear conscience seems to have had a blighting effect on the most fruitful part of his creative personality. Galich produced his most lasting work as a dissembler inside the system. His wrestling with his conscience bore creative fruit; and when the conscience found peace, the fruit dried up.

Notes

1. Lev Kopelev, "Pamiati Aleksandra Galicha," *Kontinent,* 16 (1978), 335.

2. Nataliia Rubenshtein, "Vykliuchite magnitofon—pogovorim o poete," *Vremia i my,* 2 (1975), 164.

3. Aleksandr Galich, *General'naia repetitsiia* (Frankfurt/Main, 1974), 64-7.

4. Ibid., 75.

5. A. Galich, "Kul'tura i bor'ba za prava cheloveka. Beseda s A. Galichem," *Russkaia mysl',* 3179, 24 November 1977, 7.

6. Galich, *General'naia repetitsiia,* 77.

7. Raisa Orlova, "My ne khuzhe Goratsiia," *Vremia i my,* 51 (1980), 23.

8. Viktor Nekrasov, "Sasha Galich," *Ekho,* 1 (1978), 81-2.

9. *Ocherki istorii russkoi sovetskoi dramaturgii,* ed. S. V. Vladimirov and G. A. Lapkina, II, *1934-1945* (Leningrad-Moscow, 1966), 232-3.

10. Galich, *General'naia repetitsiia,* 181.

11. Ibid., 125.

12. Michael Glenny, "The Soviet Theatre," in Robert Auty and Dimitri Obolensky (eds), *An Introduction to Russian Language and Literature* (Cambridge, 1977), 282 (*Companion to Russian Studies,* 2).

13. See Peter Yershov, *Comedy in the Soviet Theater* (New York, 1956), 238-9. Munblit's autobiographical *Rasskazy o pisateliakh* (Moscow, 1968), does not mention Galich.

14. V. Frolov, *Zhanry sovetskoi dramaturgii* (Moscow, 1957), 251-2.

15. *Sovremennaia dramaturgiia,* 6 (1958), 131-98.

16. Vladimir Maximov, *Farewell from Nowhere,* translated from the Russian by Michael Glenny (London, 1978), 262-3.

17. S. S. Mokul'sky (chief editor), *Teatral'naia entsiklopediia,* 5 vols. (Moscow, 1961-67), I (1961), col. 1087.

18. Ibid.

19. A. A. Surkov (chief editor), *Kratkaia literaturnaia entsiklopediia,* 9 vols. (Moscow, 1962-78), II (1964), col. 45.

20. S. I. Iutkevich (chief editor), *Kinoslovar'* (Moscow, 1970), II, Supplement, cols. 1071-2.

21. Iurii Krotkov, "A. Galich," *Novyi zhurnal,* 130 (1978), 242.

22. Galich, *General'naia repetitsiia,* 172.

23. Ibid., 173-4.

24. Ibid., 190.

25. Ibid., 13.

26. Ibid., 171-2.

27. Raisa Orlova, "My ne khuzhe Goratsiia," *Vremia i my,* 51 (1980), 20.

28. Ibid., 19.

29. A. Galich, "Pesnia, zhizn', bor'ba. Interv'iu Aleksandra Galicha spetsial'nym korrespondentam *Poseva* G. Raru i A. Iugovu," *Posev* (August 1974), 14-5.

30. Raisa Orlova, "My ne khuzhe Goratsiia," 11.

31. Galich, *General'naia repetitsiia,* 21.

32. Iu. Krotkov, "A. Galich," *Novyi zhurnal,* 130 (1978), 245.

33. *Ocherki istorii russkoi sovetskoi dramaturgii,* ed. S. V. Vladimirov and G. A. Lapkina, III, *1945-1967* (Leningrad, 1968), 423.

34. Ibid., 427. Some other sources indicate that Galich and Grekova co-wrote a play called *August (Avgust),* which was banned.

35. Iurii Mal'tsev, *Vol'naia russkaia literatura* (Frankfurt/Main, 1976), 85-9.

36. *Grani,* 59 (1965), 7-77; Galich's songs are on pp. 24-8.

37. Raisa Orlova, "My ne khuzhe Goratsiia," 9.

38. Galich, *General'naia repetitsiia,* 141.

39. Raisa Orlova, "My ne khuzhe Goratsiia," 8-9. See also Lev Kopelev, "Pamiati Aleksandra Galicha," *Kontinent,* 16 (1978), 336. Kopelev estimates the audience on this occasion at 1500. The dissident poet Vadim Delone was in Akademgorodok on this occasion; he reports that over the door of the club where the concert was held was a banner bearing the words: "Poets! Siberia awaits you!". Delone links Galich's experience with the Galanskov-Ginzburg trial, held in January 1968 (V. Delone, "Odinnadtsat' let tomu nazad," *Ekho,* 2-3 (1979), 181).

40. S. Grigor'ev, F. Shubin, "Eto sluchilos' na 'Svobode'," *Nedelia,* 18 (944), 17-23 April 1978, 7.

41. Orlova, 14.

42. R. (E. Romanov), "'Erika' beret chetyre kopii," *Posev,* 1 (1968), 59-61.

43. A. Galich, *Pesni* (Frankfurt/Main, 1969).

44. *Poema Rossii. Pesni o dukhovnoi svobode. Ironicheskie pesni* (Paris, 1971). The attribution to Galich is made by Archbishop John of San Francisco in his introduction to this book (5-7).

45. A. Galich, *Pokolenie obrechennykh* (Frankfurt/Main, 1972).

46. Efim Etkind, "Chelovecheskaia komediia Galicha," *Kontinent,* 5 (1975), 405-26.

47. There is a color reproduction of this picture in *Soviet Literature,* 12 (1949), frontispiece; its Russian title is *Utro Rodiny nashei.*

48. Nataliia Rubenshtein, "Vykliuchite magnitofon—pogovorim o poete," *Vremia i my,* 2(1975), 172.

49. Raisa Orlova records that Galich gave her a copy of this song as she was leaving Dubna for Moscow on 24 August 1968; that evening "my daughter Maia and her husband Pavel Litvinov came to see us, and Lev (Kopelev) read them the poem . . . And the next day, the 25th at mid-day there took place on Red Square the demonstration of protest against the invasion of Czechoslovakia. Seven people dared to go out . . . ("My ne khuzhe Goratsiia," 14-5).

50. For a fuller account of the songs in *Pokolenie obrechennykh,* see Gerry Smith, "Whispered Cry: the Songs of Alexander Galich," *Index on Censorship,* III, 3 (1974), 11-28.

51. For a general account of the genre, see G. S. Smith, "Modern Russian Underground Song: An Introductory Survey," *Journal of Russian Studies,* 28 (1974), 3-12; Gene Sosin, "*Magnitizdat:* Uncensored Songs of Dissent," in R. L. Tokes (ed.), *Dissent in the USSR: Politics, Ideology and People* (Baltimore and london, 1975), 276-309; Gerry Smith, "Underground Songs," *Index on Censorship,* VII, 2(1978), 67-72.

52. Bulat Okudzhava, *65 pesen* (Ann Arbor, 1980), 26.

53. A. Galich, "Pesnia, zhizn', bor'ba. Interv'iu . . . spetsial'nym korrespondentam *Poseva* G. Raru i A. Iugovu," *Posev,* August 1974, 13-14.

54. Ibid., 13.

55. Ibid., 14.

56. For a witty discussion of this dismal subject, see Efim Etkind, "Leonid Brezhnev kak pisatel'," *Vremia i my,* 30 (1978), 126-41.

57. *Grani,* 70 (1969), 213.

58. Leonid Vladimirov, *Rossiia bez prikras i umolchanii* (Frankfurt/Main, 2nd ed. 1969), 216-17; in the English version of this book, *The Russians* (New York-Washington-London, 1968, 184-5) the song is referred to in less detail, after discussion of *Clouds* and *Goldminer's Waltz*, but also not attributed to Galich.

59. Raisa Orlova, "My ne khuzhe Goratsiia," 8.

60. See Peter Reddaway, *Uncensored Russia* (London, 1972), 476. Solzhenitsyn has said that he and Galich were co-opted *in absentia* and without their consent (Alexander Solzhenitsyn, *The Oak and the Calf. Sketches of Literary Life in the Soviet Union,* translated by Harry Willetts (New York, 1980), 372).

61. Murray Seeger, "Russian Satirist Takes Art and Bitterness Underground," *International Herald Tribune,* 2 April 1974, 5.

62. Gene Sosin, "And Then Came Galich's Turn," *New York Times,* 12 February 1972; *Index on Censorship,* I (1972), 87.

63. On the Litfond, see Martin Dewhirst and Robert Farrell (eds), *The Soviet Censorship* (Metuchen, N. J., 1973), 43-4.

64. Galich, *General'naia repetitsiia,* 89. The entry on Arbuzov (b. 1908) in the *Concise Literary Encyclopedia (Kratkaia literaturnaia entsiklopediia,* vol. I, Aarne-Gavrilov (Moscow, 1962), 280) lists *City of the Dawn* among Arbuzov's works, and states that it was written in 1941 with a "new edition" in 1957; Galich gives the date of Arbuzov's claim as 1956 (*General'naia repetitsiia,* 88).

65. Raisa Orlova, "My ne khuzhe Goratsiia," 16.

66. For details of these signings, see *Soviet Analyst,* III, 4 (1974), 7; *Posev,* XXX, 5 (1974), 9-10; S. P. de Boer, E. J. Driessen, H. L. Verhaar (eds), *Biographical Dictionary of Dissidents in the Soviet Union, 1956-1975* (The Hague-Boston-London, 1982), 147-8.

67. Orlova, "My ne khuzhe Goratsiia," 18.

68. *General'naia repetitsiia,* 131-6.

69. Vladimir Naumov, "Tot samyi Galich, kotoryi poet pesenki," *Russkaia mysl',* 16 November 1972, No. 2921, 5. Naumov was apparently the first to publish the information that Galich had never been in either labor camp or the army.

70. Ruvim Rublev, "Galich proshchaetsia s Leningradom," *Novoe russkoe slovo,* 18 June 1980, 2.

71. Translated in Gene Sosin, "Alexander Galich: Russian Poet of Dissent," *Midstream,* XX, 4 (1974), 36.

72. Translated in Smith, "Whispered Cry . . . ," 17. There is evidence that Galich was being removed from literature before his actual expulsion from the unions. Whereas his work is given quite generous space in Vladimirov and Lapkina's history of the Soviet theater (see notes 9 and 33 above), and in other reference works (see notes 19 and 20 above), his name does not appear in *Istoriia sovetskogo dramaticheskogo teatra,* Vol. 5, *1941-1953* (Moscow, 1969); nor does he appear in the otherwise very detailed V. N. Antropov et al. (compilers), *Stsenaristy sovetskogo khudozhestvennogo kino, 1917-1967. Spravochnik* (Moscow, 1972).

73. Orlova, "My ne khuzhe Goratsiia," 18.

74. O. S., "Briusel'. Vystuplenie A. A. Galicha," *Russkaia mysl',* 26 September 1974, 9.

75. A. Galich, "Kul'tura i bor'ba za prava cheloveka. Beseda s A. Galichem," *Russkaia mysl',* No. 3179, 24 November 1977, 7.

76. Mikhail Agurskii, "Eshche raz ob Aleksandre Galiche," *Nasha strana* (Tel Aviv), 28 June 1978, 6.

77. Alexander Galich, *Bloshinyi rynok. Pochti fantasticheskii, no ne nauchnyi roman, Vremia i my,* 24 (1977), 5-54; 25 (1978), 5-54 (sic).

78. E. Romanov, "Vozvrashchenie. Pamiati Aleksandra Arkad'evicha Galicha," *Posev,* XXXIV, 2 (1978), 3.

79. "Beseda s Aleksandrom Galichem," *Issledovatel'skii otdel Radio Svoboda, Vspomogatel'nye materialy,* RS 217/74, 17 July 1974, 4 unnumbered pages, 2.

80. Ibid., 4.

81. A. Galich, "Kul'tura i bor'ba za prava cheloveka," 7.

82. Ibid.

83. Iu. Aleshin, "Vopreki interesam razriadki. Radiodiversanty imperializma," *Pravda,* 13 January 1976, 4.

84. Unsigned report, *Literaturnaia gazeta,* May 1976.

85. V. B. Kassis, L. S. Kolosov, M. A. Mikhailov, B. A. Piliatskin, *Poimany s polichnym* (Moscow, 1976), 23.

86. V. B. Kassis, L. S. Kolosov, M. A. Mikhailov, B. A. Piliatskin, *Sovershenno sekretno* (Moscow, 1977), 49.

87. CND/Reuter report, CN 112, 20 December 1977.

88. Radio Liberty report, No. 529, 16 December 1977, 1.

89. Ibid., 3.

90. A. Galich, *Kogda ia vernus'* (Frankfurt/Main, 1977), 124.

91. S. Grigor'ev, F. Shubin, "Eto sluchilos' na 'Svobode'," *Nedelia,* 18 (944), 17-23 April 1978, 6-7.

92. Mikhail Agurskii, "Eshche raz ob Alexandre Galiche," *Nasha strana* (Tel Aviv), 28 June 1978, 6.

93. On Grossman's life, see most recently Boris Zaks, "Nemnogo o Grossmane," *Kontinent,* 26 (1980), 352-63.

94. "Beseda s pisatelem Vasiliem Aksenovym," *Kontinent,* 27 (1981), 433-45.

95. Vladimir Maximov, "Do svidaniia, Sasha," *Russkaia mysl',* No 3184, 29 December 1977, 2.

96. R. Daniel'son, "I kazhdyi priiut, kak khram...," *Golem* (Studencheskoe ob"edinenie Ierusalim), n.d., (17-22), 21-2.

97. On Galich's songs as "theater for one actor" see Lev Ventsov (pseud., i.e., Boris Shragin), "Poeziia A. Galicha," *Vestnik russkogo studencheskogo khristianskogo dvizheniia,* 104-5 (II-III), (1972), 211-28; Galich himself stated that he was moving away from this concept in his recent work when he was interviewed in 1974 (A. Galich, "Pesnia, zhizn', bor'ba... (see note 29 above), 13). The idea was put forward again in Andrei Siniavskii, "Teatr Galicha," *Vremia i my,* 14 (1977), 142-50, an article that contains some brilliant insights.

A Note on the Translations

These translations were begun in the hope that someone would sing them to guitar accompaniment using Galich's original tunes, and singability in this context has been a powerful influence on the choice of words. Within this constraint, the intention has of course been to transmit as much as possible of the meanings of the originals as the resources of the translator's wit will allow.

Translating Galich presents problems above and beyond those stemming from the fact that his words are meant to be sung. His subject matter is so closely enmeshed with Soviet reality that there can be no real question of translating him so as to read as if the text had originally been conceived in English. To take the most obvious things, his texts are heavily studded with place-names, personal names, the titles of social institutions, and so on right down to tiny details of clothes and food; it is these things that give the songs their immediacy, their tight grip on Soviet social reality. And they are as untranslatable as the atmosphere in which the songs were conceived and performed. The songs were written out of a culture which it is a relief to declare alien, and though they were written in opposition to the official mainstream of that culture, they remain essentially part of it. And so, regrettably but unavoidably, some notes on the texts have to be supplied.

Galich's verse forms present problems of a different kind for the translator. Metrical organization as highly regulated as his is not, of course, a widespread feature in modern English verse. But even in the Russian context Galich's forms are unusual; he does not use the standard meters and stanza forms of literary verse, but has developed a repertoire of his own. The meter of the Klim Petrovich cycle, for example, has been used only rarely by other poets, but for Galich it is a staple narrative form. The decision to try and make the texts singable to the original tunes has necessitated isometric translation, and an attempt has also been made to retain where possible Galich's rhyme schemes. The result is bound to be somewhat odd in the context both of English verse and of the growing number of isometric translations of Russian literary verse. But the ultimate test of these translations will come only if they are ever taken off the page and sung, like their great originals.

The Russian texts of all the songs and poems translated here are contained in Alexander Galich, *Kogda ya vernus'. Polnoe sobranie stikhov i pesen* (Frankfurt, 1981). The arrangement of the songs and the division into sub-sections in this book, however, has not necessarily been retained.

Songs of Many Colors

Lenochka

One night in April, Lenochka
Was standing at her post,
This gorgeous girl with chestnut hair
Was standing at her post.
So pretty and so proud she was,
She stood out in the crowd;
Right on the city boundary
She stood there at her post.

The thing a copper's got to do
Is curse the whole day through,
The nice ones and the bossy ones
Must curse the whole day through;
She'd rather go out on the town
Sniffing a lilac bloom,
But she those nasty car drivers
Must curse the whole day through.

So there she stood, our Lenochka,
A sergeant on the force,
She grew up in Ostankino,
This sergeant on the force;
Now some folk have expense accounts,
We all use what we've got,
But Lenochka, our Lenochka's
A sergeant on the force.

Then suddenly there caught her eye
Some headlights coming fast,
Away from Sheremetevo
Some headlights coming fast;
With sirens blaring throatily—
Pedestrians scattered fast,
At Lena drove these foreigners
Their headlights coming fast.

But Lenochka, she waved them down,
Her hand it didn't shake,
Her knees were rather wobbly,
But her hand, it didn't shake;
The cars weren't taxis on the prowl
But they all hit their brakes,

The cheeky cow, she waved them down,
Her hand it didn't shake.

So, suddenly the leading car,
It started slowing down;
It wasn't a burst or anything,
But it started slowing down;
The heavies from the KGB
Around it in a crowd;
But as it got to Lenochka
It started to slow down.

And in that car with heraldry—
An Ethiopian beau,
He stared and stared at Lenochka,
This Ethiopian beau;
And, rising from the leather seat
(So's not to miss his throw)—
He tossed her a chrysanthemum,
This Ethiopian beau!

Next morning came a messenger—
CC CPSU,
His motorbike a special make—
CC CPSU;
He waved his cap at Lenochka,
He was in such a stew,
"You're wanted, Miss Potapova—
CC CPSU!"

And there at Party headquarters—
The Ethiopian;
They'd rolled out the red carpets for
The Ethiopian;
He made a speech of gratitude
And wiped his noble brow;
For he was of the royal blood,
This Ethiopian.

His suite had drained their vodka down,
But he looks at the door,
His souvenir pennant in his hand,
He's looking at the door.
An ally welcomed on all sides,

But he just puffs and blows—
Then there was heard an orchestra
And they opened up the door;

In tulle and panne all radiant,
She came into the hall,
And everybody gasped out "Ah!"
When she came in the hall.
The handsome sprig of royalty
Achmed Ali-Pasha
Exclaimed "I say, that's made my day!"
When she came into the hall.

And soon our little Lenochka
Was known the whole world o'er;
This maiden from Ostankino
Was known the whole world o'er;
When Achmed did his daddy in
And got himself the throne,—
Sharina L. Potapova
Was known the whole world o'er!

A Ballad About
Conscientiousness

Yegor Petrovich Maltsev
Was ailing really bad,—
Life going out of fingers
And going out of glands.

Out of his other members
His life was going as well,
It looked as if before long
There would be nothing left.

When like a herd of cattle
His local inlaws come,
Of all that poor Yegor was,
What will be left for them?

There'll just be one old raincoat,
A pillow for the bed,
One book, one savings bank book,
Worth just a couple of quid.

One bowl, one pair of saucepans,
One torn subscription form,
A used-up season ticket
For buses, trains and trams.

That's all, Yegor has left us,
A man's been here and gone!
And the obituary column
Will tell us of it soon.

Now kids can eat their doughnuts,
And drink their soda pop,
But with his diabetes
They'd poison him, full stop.

Yegor's in bed and sleeping,
He hardly weighs a gram,
And hardly even breathing,
He sees a wondrous dream:

A hall that's large and handsome,
Too grand to comprehend,
And there Yegor is lying,
With flags and wreaths behind,

And his enormous portrait
All bathed in crimson light,
But he'd got no idea
If he was still alive.

He blinked away the midges
As if he wasn't dead,
But though he did this blinking
He couldn't turn his head.

The atmosphere was stuffy,
Just like a public bath,
And he was more a dead man
Than someone still alive.

But in chorus o'er Yegor did sing
The Soviet Army Choir,
And Soviet-Army-chorusing,
They sang "Stand up, Yegor!

Stand up, Yegor Petrovich,
Stand up as tall as tall,
Come on, Yegor Petrovich,
Answer your country's call!

One of our big newspapers
Has given the world the news
That in the Soviet Union
Diabetes has been cured!

You see, old chap, it's something
Where you can't make a mess,
For you would be insulting
Your native country's press."

At this, our comrade Maltsev
He sat up in his bed,
With life no longer going
Out of his finger ends.

He washes out his undies
And tucks the blankets in,
Into his bloodstream courses
Dissolving insulin ...

And through the squares of Moscow
Strides out this friend of ours,
Now everything's available
That he can see around!

Now he can try those sweeties,
And drink that soda fizz,—
It's only Soviet power
Can make things work like this!

This Terrifying Century

Monday afternoon, and I felt awful sick,
Had a splitting headache I could hardly bear;
Off I went to see the garage orderly,
Told him I just had to get away somewhere.

Asked him if he'd let me have a travel form,
Somewhere way up north, as far as possible.
Then he asked me if I hadn't had a few,
"No I haven't, I'm just feeling rotten, see?

I was at this wedding most of yesterday,
Had a bit to eat but didn't pig myself,
But I wouldn't drink a toast to Ksenia,
Didn't wet my whistle, just was sitting there.

I didn't touch a glassful, not the tiniest,
All I did was sit and chew a crust of bread,
Looking at that four-eyed smart-arse Ksenia'd wed,
Making himself out to be a scientist.

Who's to say I haven't done some studying?
Maybe I'm a driver just by accident!
I could see the others, they all drunk it in,
As for Ksenia, she sat there and lapped it up.

He was like a bishop at communion,
Preaching about Xs, sines and logarithms,
Tarted up in this here brand new suit of his,
Made to measure, you could tell it cost a bit.

He's not one of your real atom scientists,
He just works at some old crappy institute,
Tries to make out he's in charge (my eye he is)
Of some electronical computer thing.

Says that he can tell this thing to multiply
25 by 9 point zero-zero-one,
All he does is press a knob, and shut his eyes,
Sits there skiving while the thing completes the job.

There I was, and I was feeling choked as hell,
I stood up. I don't know what got into me,

65

And suggested we all wet the baby's head,
People didn't get it,—I'm sure Ksenia did.

Though the night was young I made my exit then,
Slammed the door and let them all get on with it,
I was feeling what you might call vexed to hell,
But I made it to the tube and tottered in.

Like an offering on a church collection plate,
Penny in the automatic barrier,—
But the automatic bloody entrance gate
Shut on me and ripped my bloody pants to shreds.

That was it, I can't remember anything,
Tears came to my eyes, I started kicking out,
Then the cops came, whistling fit to wake the dead,
Everybody laughed at my predicament . . .

Sign me out a car then, mate,—be human, please,
Then I'll drive away till I get sent for trial,
I'm pissed off with everything to do with this
Automatic bastard of a century!"

The Right To A Holiday

Grabbed some bathtub vodka and some halva too,
Couple of Riga beers and herrings from Crimea,
And I set off to the Moscow mental home
For a visit to the loonies and our kid.

> Oh, a loony's life would suit anyone,
> Kip down when you want, sing if songs you want!
> Every one of them's got some privilege,
> Some by Stalin, and some by Hitler given.

So my brother meets me in the corridor,
And I get a telling-off for being late;
Says he, "let's crack the vodka for a start,
It's the loonies' noonday rest hour," he says.

> Schizophrenics making brooms and mats,
> Parano-i-acs doodling Os on pads,
> And the ones who were only nervous types
> Were asleep in bed, far as I could tell.

When we'd had a little drink to get going,
My brother started getting very sad,
Said he'd go and slit the head shrink's throat—
Wouldn't let him go to Moscow, the prat.

> For in Moscow my bro had a lot to do,
> Like getting his pension money through,
> And in Moscow too was his legal wife,
> (And another certain lady on the side).

Then we had the herrings, washed 'em down with beer,
And we scoffed the halva too for something sweet,
And my brother says to me: "Listen here,
Why don't you stand in for me for a bit?

> In the way we walks and our ugly dials,
> You and me have always had sim'lar styles,
> And in Moscow you're always on the go,
> You could live here like in a nursing home!"

Off he takes his slippers and his dressing gown,
And he ruffles up my hair a little bit,

That there dressing gown went on me like a glove,
Just as if it had been specially made to fit!

    Then he grabbed my coat, left to catch the train,
    And I pinned my money around my waist,
    And then off I stroll for everyone to see,
    After all, what's wrong with a holiday?

The wide world is quiet and still, all is peace;
And I stroll about and think, very cool:
Should I be the president of the US,
Or just graduate from Advanced Party School?

    Oh, a loony's life would suit anyone,
    Kip down when you want, sing if songs you want!
    Every one of us has got some privilege,
    Some by Stalin, and some by Hitler given!

The Ballad of Surplus Value

> "... A spectre is haunting Europe,
> the spectre of Communism ..."

Now I've coddled my marxist scholasticals,
Even gleaning the meaning of periods;
Keeping close to the commas, not like numskulls do,
Studied *Capital* and *Anti-During* too.
Unabashed by my vast masculinity,
I've dressed as the spectre for festivals;
Everywhere, both out loud and in writing too,
I've declared the whole shooting match right and true.

No ifs and buts, no ifs and buts, no ifs and buts,
Maybe I'm nuts, but who's not nuts? So you're not nuts?

But I'll tell you what happened some days ago:
I decided to buy a new radio.
And on my day off for an hour or so
Settled down to give ear to the orchestra.
They were playing that what-d'you-call opera
Where Carmen gives her man the old heave-ho,
And after we'd had Escamilio—
Heard a surname that sounded familio,

Now what the deuce, now what the deuce, now what the deuce?
So who's amused, I'm not amused, are you amused?

The announcer said "Citizen (naming me)
Your old auntie has died in Fingalia,
And for you an appointment is imminent—
Foreign Office (Department Juridical)!"
I was on my hind legs like a stallion—
Keep it down, for Pete's sake put a sock in it!
It's a subject that's always a tricky one—
It's not marxist, not one little bit it ain't!

Disgrace and shame, disgrace and shame, disgrace and shame,
And when I'd nearly made my name! You've made your name?

I was tossing and turning the whole night through,
That old bag of an auntie had cooked my goose!
And the missus was weeping and worrying,

69

Maybe Stalin's passed on, but you never know!
Packed my bag—soap and towel and underpants,
If they kept me I'd not have to go without!
When I got there, my guts were all jellified,
But they treated me just like a gentleman!

Ha-ha, clap-clap, ha-ha, clap-clap, ha-ha, clap-clap,
But I just stood and shut my trap. You've shut your trap?

The first thing we had was a conference,
They read my aunt's last will and testament:
"I, the undersigned (surname and christian name),
Being of sound mind and body, et cetera,
Do bequeath all my land and the factory
—Not to hubby (that shit of a lady's man)—
Let my favorite nephew, Volodechka,
Have the lot, and I wish him a lot of luck!"

I don't mind that, I don't mind that, I don't mind that!
It looks as if I'll pack my bag! You've packed your bag?

Well, that Friday I got to the offices,
Told the bosses just where they could stuff the thing;
Says I, nice t'have made your acquaintances,
But I don't need your fiddling pittance now!
And I went on the booze the whole weekend through,
Little kip, and straight back on the booze again,
And I toasted my motherland (*ex-*, that is),
And my auntie's eternal memory.

I swilled and swilled, then got the bill, then got the bill;
Don't want the score, I want some more! You want some more?

In the name of my dear late lamented aunt,
Blued the last I'd got left in my bank account;
So I got up to go, but my drinking mates
To a man they all reached for their pocketbooks.
"Oh, come on now, you treasure, you lovely man,
Go ahead and permit us to loan you some!
We can settle up later all friendly-like,
You can send us a bit of your leftovers."

So that's the way, I thank you all! I thank you all!
I'll send you all some foreign clothes! You'll get some clothes!

Well, I borrowed a thousand all told, I did,
Pay you back? Lord be praised, I'm not short of it!
And that thou. went right down, with my compliments—
And the restaurant started to stomp, oh yes,
That nice bass-player gave me his bow to wear,
And we drank top-class booze, not the ordinary;
And a couple of ladies, all permed and set,
Kept on saying that I was their precious pet.

We drank all day, we drank all night, another night,
Well, I don't mind, and you don't mind, we all don't mind.

That whole week from Sunday to Sunday night,
We were having a really fantastic time,
It was Monday before I came back to earth,
And I sat down to look at a telly show.
The announcer droned on about progress made
In the Soviet conquest of outer space,—

And then: "Now the news from abroad. Revolution in Fingalia! The first
decree of the people's government enacts the total nationalization of land,
factories, railways and all other industrial enterprises. The peoples of the
Soviet Union send greetings to the fraternal people of Fingalia and
congratulate them on their magnificent victory!"

The sight of the screen made me want to spew,
What in hell do you mean, it's all nationalized?!
It's *mine,* it belongs to my aunt and me,
That's why I was off to Fingalia!
You're a bunch of old rogues and clever dicks!
And it's all got to do with your marxist tricks!
There's no tale in the world that's sadder
Than the story of surplus value!

I've had enough, I've had enough, I've had enough!
And now I'm absolutely nuts! But who's not nuts?!

The Red Triangle

Well, there's nothing I can say, is there, really?
Here I stand before you, like a naked infant,
I admit that I've been courting Pasha's Nina,
Took her round the park and to the Pekin restaurant,

And I bought the lass a nice perlon roll-on,
And I took her round the Kremlin exhibition;
At the time, my wife (that's Comrade Paramonov)
Was away abroad on some official business.

She got back to find a poison-pen letter,
With a photo of yours truly with Nina;
I woke up next day and found that my better
Half had took her things and gone, no explaining!

       Off she'd gone,
       I tell you, off she'd gone!

So I went to her at Union headquarters,
Said she'd done for me, I got down and grovelled,
"That slut Nina's nothing all that important,
Let me off, my dear Comrade Paramonov!"

She went black as night and wouldn't stop yelling,
"Oh! I've heard all that before—cut the weeping!
No use eating humble pie,—you'll be telling
Everything what's happened at the Party meeting!"

First she screamed and then she shook, started squeaking,
All the smoothies gathered round with valerian,
That Tamara Sixinhand and Johnny Twitcher,
And that adviser that they say's "from the ministry."

       Just like that,
       I tell you, just like that!

Fair enough then, so I go to the meeting,
Now I think, it was the first of November,
I made sure to get a sickness certificate
And prescription from the nurse (she didn't like it).

There sat Paramonov in a brand new headscarf,
When she saw me, she turned red as a beetroot,
The first item down was "Freedom for Africa,"
—I came later, under "Any Other Business."

During Ghana, folks sneaked out to buy sausage,
Wouldn't have minded some myself—couldn't afford it;
I was trembling like a leaf when they called me,
"Right, let's have it, lad, the lot, the whole story!"

          Everything,
          I tell you, everything!

Well, there's nothing I can say, is there, really?
Here I stand before you like a naked infant,
I admit that I've been courting Pasha's Nina,
We've been round the park, and out for Chinese dinner.

I confessed the rotten West had been sapping
The foundations of my moral conceptions,
"What the hell," I said, "you know these things happen!
All in all," says I, "least said, soonest mended!"

Read my sick note saying I'm a bit mental,
And I did my best to milk them for pity;
They were glad, they said, to see I'd repented:
—Severe Reprimand (recorded in the minutes).

          Oh dear me,
          I tell you, oh dear me!

Straightaway I bought the nicest flowers available,
And I waited at the bosses' special doorway;
Paramonov she stalked out and turned navy,
Swept off in her big black car, left me gawping!

So I shot back in and went to the cloakroom,
Said to Pasha I'd be coming round that evening;
"Not so fast," says she, " 'Immoral conduct'
On your Party card means you won't be welcome!

And my nice young niece, *Miss* Nina, I'd bargain,
Would agree exactly with that assessment,

She's sold all the veg. she came to market,
And departed for her res., as intended."

How 'bout that?
I tell you, how 'bout that?

So I write the local Party a letter,
Ask them if I can drop round (personal matter);
I arrive, and sitting there is my better
Half, she turned as white as a spectre.

Side by side we're sitting in the Party office,
And the lady says, all smiling and pleasant,
"Well, he's had his reprimand, so let's drop it,
Now the pair of you should make up and mend things."

So we waltzed out side by side from the office,
Arm in arm to the Pekin for celebrations,
And we drank a toast (her wine, and me vodka)
To our model Soviet family relations!

That's the lot . . .

Episodes from the Life of Klim Petrovich Kolomiitsev, Workshop Foreman, Holder of Many Orders, Deputy of the Town Soviet

Episode One
In which Klim Petrovich addresses a Meeting in Defense of Peace

You can go and ask the missus (that's Dasha),
You can go and ask her sister (that's Klavka),
I was steady as a rock, not a tremor,
(Maybe just the teeniest little bit hung over).

I was doing what you're s'posed to do on Sundays:
I had soaped and steamed meself in the bathhouse;
When the family arrived, about lunchtime,
We began to wet our whistles and tell stories.

I had took one little tot, to get going,
And I swear it was a small one, so help me!
When a car drives up and stops at our gateway,
I could tell it was official from the number.

Out I goes to see to what we owes the honor,
(Could have been the KGB, you never know it);
—It was only a penpusher from the office,
"In you get," says he, "come on, let's get going."

Well, if it's me they're asking for, then oops-a-daisy!
There's a peace defense service at the clubhouse,
And Number One was there and other high-ups.

So I sits down on the penpusher's lap then,
And he shoves a piece of paper in my fingers;
"Have a look" says he, "during the journey
At your speech—it's really most impressive."

Fair enough, I thinks, I'll add to my credit,
Thank the Lord, I'm no chicken at these speeches,
When we got there, I mounted the platform,
All polite, sat down away from the middle.

And I see the chairman wink for my attention,
'Sif to say, go and speak for the workers;

Up I get, and, not all jerky like a rattle,
I speak out very sternly and slowly:

"Those accursed Israeli warmongers
Are known the whole world over.
As a woman and a mother, I say to you:
I demand they be called to order!

I've been a widow many years—
My life's not easy,
But the sacred cause of peace
I'd die defending!

As a woman, as a mother I declare to you . . ."
When I said it, my jaw dropped, I'll tell you,
It's the sort of cockup that can happen!
That young bastard of an office-boy, the smartarse
Got his knickers in a twist and mixed the scripts up.

Couldn't decide if I should stop or continue,
But no boos came from the hall, and no tittering;
Number One, I noticed, wasn't pulling faces—
He was sitting there and nodding approval.

So I set off at a gallop through the phrases
(Thank the Lord, they're never any different!)—
When I finished, everybody started clapping,
Number One put his personal palms together.

Afterwards he called me into his sanctum,
And he said to me so everyone could hear it:
"Well done, lad! That was spoken like a worker!
You correctly analyzed the situation!"

Bit of an annoying story, that . . .

Episode Two
In which Klim Petrovich tries to get his section awarded the distinction "Workshop of Communist Labor," and when he gets nowhere, goes on the booze

In the office they all laughed and said I'd made it,
With my extra living space and king-size wages;
But I wasn't going to drop it! "Come on, comrades,
It's not *that* crap that I'm after, see, it's *justice!*

What I'm after's for my whole bloody section
To get credit, not just me as the foreman,
It's the whole socialist camp we're strengthening,
Our production level's always higher than normal!

And I'm bound to say I don't think it's funny,
And I'd like to know exactly who's behind it,
When you never give a badge of distinction
To a section as exemplary as mine is!"

But everyone says, all my mates they say
(That's Frol and Pakhomov and Tonka)—
Can't be done, says they, no way, says they,
It's dead tricky, says they, dead tricky.

Get stuffed!, says I, Up your arses!, says I,
I'll go, says I, to the Party, says I.

But the local Party office too said "Steady,
That's enough of all this long-faced bellyaching,
You're a Party member, not some stupid neddy,
Men like you should understand the situation!

Don't forget the foreign press is always knocking
Everything that's going on here on our side,
If you think the Yanks are dozing, you're mistaken,
In the effing Pentagon they're on the lookout!"

But I had my answer pat, I got sarky:
"If it's go-slow that you want, you can have it!
If you'd like to know how we supply the market,—
We're on 1990's output now, God dammit!"

Come off it!, says they, Cut the crap!, says they,
Enough of this cursing and swearing,
Pipe down!, says they, Shut your trap!, says they,
Sit tight!, says they, Grin and bear it!

But me, says I, I'm pissed off, says I,
I'm taking this right to the top, says I.

But in Moscow I get treated like a beggar,
I get shunted from one desk to another,
"Course, you're right, they say, dead right, but however,
At the present time it's rather awkward, brother.

What would happen if your shop took the notion,
Volunteered to go for special output targets?
Just you think!—d'nt take much imagination,—
What the BBC would have to say, the bastards!"

Then they mentioned my awards and my floor space,
And they showed me to the door, "Nice t'have met you,
If the world position wasn't quite so complex,
We'd be glad to give your workshop a medal!

But the thing, says they (though you're right, says they,
Your production couldn't be higher)—,
But, but, says they, it's not flags, they say,
What you're turning out's *barbed bloody wire!*"

If that's, says I, how it is, says I,
I'm off, says I, on the piss, says I.
And I was.

Episode Three
In which Klim Petrovich protests against economic aid to the underdeveloped
countries

This is a very tragic tale, one which Klim Petrovich narrates in a state of
extreme annoyance, and therefore permits himself certain rather unparlia-
mentary turns of phrase . . .

Was just aiming to survive, I'm no hero,
But my guts were feeling like pickled onions!
There we were, flogging all round Algeria,
Delegated from the Board of our Trade Union.

78

All them meetings, all them speeches slating NATO,
I was shagged, and I was getting bloody hungry,
Wouldn't touch their frogs hind legs with a bargepole!
Seem to think that I'm a Chink, stupid sugars!

Chairman Mao (up his armhole) couldn't have stuck it,
I'm no hero, as I said, and I'm not greedy;
But the missus'd put some tins in my luggage,
Bless her heart, she understands I need feeding!

Trouble was, she'd had to rush, and she'd packed me
All there was around the shops—salted mackerel;
And as soon as I gets back to the Palace
(Shitty dump) I says "Praise be unto Allah,"
Locks myself up in my cell, and gets cracking,
Gets stuck into a few tins of salted mackerel.

Dry as dust, some bloody thirst, come next morning,
Could have drunk a pint of piss, ne'mind water!
I survived, but never again, so come night time,
I went shopping—after all, Christ almighty,
I'm not Lenin the immortal, I'd be nackered
If I had to eat some more salted mackerel!

In the shop, like a spare knob at a wedding,
I went hot and cold, my God, I was sweating,
It's not every day you get foreign money,
Shit! To blow the stuff on food isn't funny!

Did a tour around the store, saw some stuff there,
Hidden right out on one side, little thin tins,
But the printing on the tins wasn't in Russian,
And I'm hopeless at the local bloody lingo.

So I goes up to a fair senorita,
"Parleyvoo," says I, "Excuse, bitte-twitter,
Fill me in, have them there tins got meat in?"
And the sod gave me a nod, stupid shithouse.

So I bought some, and I felt I was floating,
I came round when I got back to the flophouse,
Down I squats on that there cot, gets my clothes off,
And I man my trusty can bloody opener.

All night through the air was blue, I effed and blinded,
Cursed and swore right through till dawn, I went crackers,
Cos that tin that I'd got in didn't have meat in,
Just my luck, it was effing salted mackerel!

That's not enough—the bloody stuff had been 'made in'
Where d'you think?—Not in Brazil or in Dublin,—
Little letters on the edge of the label,
'Leningrad, USSR', price in roubles!

Charity begins at home, and for muggins,
You can stuff your bleeding overseas missions!
Jesus Christ, we're sending aid to these sugars,
When it's us who're suffering, us starving Russians!!!

Thought before, I'm off abroad, that's not bad then,
Didn't think that I'd land up going mad there!
I found out they're just a shower of thieving muckers,
And they take plain Russian folk for foreign suckers!
I can tell you, life abroad's bloody lousy,
Even ... Even (pardon me) worse than ours is ...

Generation of the Accursed

Guignol Farce

All those shits and all those bloodsuckers
Guzzling, boozing, making trouble,
—Just on schoolbooks here you're forking out
Every month nigh on a rouble!
Silly Lucy's getting hitched quite soon,
Nothing you can do to please her!
Poor old daddy's got six kids to feed,
And they've all got to be thought of,—

    There's always this to buy, and there's that to buy,
    There's no trimmings and no luxury,
    Even cheese or sausage to go with your tea—
    It's a little here, it's a little there,
    Where's it coming from?

Silly Lucy's always giggling,
Thinks that life's a field of clover;
And Nikita, that's the littlest,
He'll get colic any moment!
Daddy hitched his braces up a notch,
With a sad smile he departed,
Went and put an application in
At the public loans department,

    'Cos there's this to buy, and there's that to buy,
    There's no trimmings and no luxury,
    Even cheese or sausage to go with your tea—
    It's a little here, it's a little there,
    Where's it coming from?

Daddy made his statement tearfully,
Waited anxious for the verdict;
The committee pondered seriously,
Their decision was as follows:
"We'd have liked so much to help you, but
Catching Uncle Sam costs money!
Your request's refused, for reasons given,
But we're sorry, insofar as

    There's always this to buy, and there's that to buy,
    There's no trimmings and no luxury,

Even cheese or sausage to go with your tea—
It's a little here, it's a little there,
Where's it coming from?

Daddy went out and got plastered then,
Gave it Lucy in the kisser,
Then when it got late on Saturday
Hanged himself from the light fitting . . .

Oh, it's not first aid that we require,
What we really need is slow aid!
So the doctor cut his braces down,
"Death, twelve p.m.," his diagnosis . . .
This man's death was unremarkable,
There was nobody left grieving,
He left nothing but a suicide note
Propped up on the television,

"There was this and that I'd have liked to buy,
There's no trimmings and no luxury,
Even cheese or sausage to go with your tea—
It's a little here, it's a little there,
Where's it coming from?"

Clouds

Oh, the clouds go by, floating by,
Like in films they float, soft and slow;
I'm chewing chicken (spiced and fried),
And my brandy's running low.

Floating clouds sail off to the east,
Soft and slow they float, soft and slow;
I bet that they're warm as toast,
But me, I've been chilled to the bone!

Once I froze like iron to ice,
Digging roads with a pick in my hand!
I left twenty long years of my life
Back in those bloody labor camps.

I can see that frozen snow-crust,
Hear the cursing when we were frisked . . .
Hey, waiter!—pineapple chunks,
And another double of this!

Rolling clouds go by, sailing far
To that dear old home in the east,
They don't know what an amnesty's for,
They don't need any lawyer to plead.

Now I'm living a life without care,
Twenty years flew straight past like a dream;
Here I sit like a lord in this bar,
And I've even still got a few teeth!

Clouds roll by to the morning sun,
With no pension, no trouble or strife;
As for me, well, twice a month,
I collect what's mine by right.

And on those two days, just like me,
Half this country sits in the bars!
And the clouds roll by to the east,
Rolling by in all of our hearts . . .

And those clouds roll by to the east,
Rolling by in all of our hearts . . . .

Hospital Gypsy Song

It was booze made my boss talk of Stalin's days,
And he wouldn't stop grabbing the wheel,
So that later the ambulance men carted us
Where the notice says "Accidents Here."
Took my pants and my old army coat away,
And they stuffed all my things in a sack,
Then along came Marusya the orderly
With a pill to put me on my back.

    I told them that I wasn't hurt,
    But if I was, and all that stuff,
    Then in this best of possible worlds
    I'm sick and tired, I've had enough,
    I've had enough, I've long been tired
    Of everything.

There was I on my cot like a mental case,
With the angel of death hovering nigh,
But my boss, he belongs to a better race,
Gets a ward to himself, nice as pie.
It's got curtains a nurse puts up specially,
He gets personal service, the swine,
He gets seen by a Jewish professor
And has parcels sent in from his wife.

    With caviar and even wine,
    And cheese, and all that sort of stuff;
    But me, I get the hospital shite,
    Though I don't care, I've had enough,
    Though I resign, I've long been tired
    Of everything.

From the jelly they give me at dinner time
I save some for the ward sister's kid,
Though I know that I'm in for a thin old time;
I'm not getting the same as his nibs!
And I've driven that sod of a boss of mine
In his limousine all over town,
You're fine fellers, the best bosses possible,
Pride and joy of this country of ours!

86

He might be a number one or two,
Etcetera, all that sort of stuff,
But I'm no worse than all his crew,
And I think rank's a load of guff,
"I'm higher than you"—it makes me spew
Like everything.

I put on my pajamas next morning time,
And I'm off for a smoke on the sly;
Who comes by?—It's Marusya the orderly,
"Hello, love! Where've you been all my life?
Be so kind as to tell me what's going on!"
—It knocked me for six, her reply:
"I'm afraid your old boss is a goner, love,
Had a heart attack during the night."

And things went on in all the wards,
And noise, and all that sort of stuff,
But I just stood there lost for words,
I felt as if I'd had enough,
All sudden I was sick and tired
Of everything.

OK, so we're not in the army now,
But I'll tell you that in the front line
That old coat of mine covered my boss and me,
And not only on just the odd night,
We've supped vodka together from billycans,
We've been roasted by enemy fire,
No, my lads, you can bet that I've little chance
Of replacing that boss who's just died!

Me crying? No, it's just those drops,
And all that blessed sort of stuff,
I've had my lot, I've had my lot,
I've really had more than enough.
I've had my lot, I've had my lot
Of everything!

The Error

We're buried out somewhere near Narva,
    Near Narva, near Narva,
We're buried out somewhere near Narva,
    We lived—and we died;
We lie as we marched,—twos together,
    Together, together,
We lie as we marched,—twos together,
    We've all had our lot.

Neither foe nor reveille disturb us,
    Disturb us, disturb us,
Neither foe nor reveille disturb us
    Stiff-frozen lads,
Except once we heard—or we thought so
    We thought so, we thought so,
Except once we heard—or we thought so
    Trumpets sounding again.

Up you get, so-and-so's, let's have you,
    Let's have you, let's have you!
Up you get, so-and-so's, let's have you,
    For blood still is blood!
If Russia is calling her fallen,
    Her fallen, her fallen,
If Russia is calling her fallen   .
    Things must be real bad!

Up we got in our crosses and chevrons,
    Our chevrons, our chevrons,
Up we got in our crosses and chevrons,
    In the smoke of the snow;
We look round, and we see it's an error,
    An error, an error,
We look round, and we see it's an error,
    We're no use at all!

Where in '43 fell the foot soldiers,
    Foot soldiers, foot soldiers,
Where in '43 fell the foot soldiers
    For nothing, in vain,—
Merry over the snow go the hunters,
    The hunters, the hunters,

Merry over the snow go the hunters,
    The hunting horns sound!

Where in '43 fell the foot soldiers,
Where in '43 fell the foot soldiers,—
Merry over the snow go the hunters,
    The hunting horns sound!

Stalin

"Jesus Christ goes on before"
Alexander Blok

Chapter 1: The Nativity

Things were all going as planned, if rather hurried:
The babe slept in its cradle; evening coming;
The extras shuffled shyly to the set;
The Holy Mother silently attending
The star of Glad Tidings as it descended
Into the stony sky of Bethlehem.
But then two swineherds burst into the byre
And shouted out that something had misfired,
That celebration day was off, alas,
That Romans didn't have a sense of humor.
The Magi turned up just at the wrong moment,
And copped two weeks inside for all their pains.

        It got very quiet,
        Lips were frozen in a shout,
        And the star hissed like a firework,
        Then it simply fizzled out.
        It got very very chilly;
        Feeling that the end was near,
        All the insects started clucking
        And the ox began to bleat.
        There was snoring, there was wailing,
        But oblivious to the din
        Was the baby in its cradle
        Blowing kisses as it slept.

Already dawn was near, the sky pink-glowing,
When right beside the stable rang out loudly
Deliberately heavy-weighted steps.
The Holy Mother froze in alarmed terror
As the door opened, and across the threshold
Appeared a pair of long Caucasian boots.
And centuries, seconds and saturnalia
Immediately stripped of all their meaning
Into a perfect circle closed up fast
As in he came; a token inclination,

And without hurrying, towards the cradle
He turned the smallpox-spatterings of his face.

> "Here we have Him, then, none other,
> Sorry stepson of the earth,
> Who with blood and with hosannas
> Comes to match himself with me . . .
> In your cradle gently burbling,
> Surely you can't be the person
> Who for days and years on end
> Will turn my life into a hell?
> Is it us, my little tiny,
> Time will toss into his scales?"
> And his moustache parted slightly
> As he gave an evil smirk.

The three wise men were pining in confinement.
It didn't take very long to break their spirit;
They caught it in the forehead and the gut;
The Roman heavy, slavering for a medal,
Said "For a start, confess, you rotten beggars,
And then we'll sort things out and see what's what."
Because they knew what happens to the fallen,
The Magi gabbled every sort of fable;
They mentioned dates and also mentioned names,
And heads began to roll. These things we've stated
Presented a most weighty indication
That this had been the start of a new age.

Chapter 2: The Leader's Oath

"Sweaty Jews with great big ugly faces,
Out for your own ends, you thieving scum,
You assorted Johns and various Matthews,
You'd do anything but tell the truth.
Rub salt in their wounds and they just love it,
They don't care, if Sinai's the reward.
Right then, I'm not going to interrupt You,—
You came first, so you can have first word.
On Your feet, go off through towns and hamlets,
Make your miracles and parables.
Tell me, Lord, why are You so unhappy?

Where have all Your fellow-warriors flown?
They were there for lodging and for supper,
But when things got bad, there's not one left.
Not for nothing that night in the garden
You turned yellow and asked to be let off.
Your rabble of sycophants—tell me, where are they
At Your fatal final hour down here?
And You're being laughed at by Barabbas—
Let him try and have a laugh at me!
You were nothing more than a precursor,
Victim of events, and not their Will,
Son of man are You, and not God's firstborn,
If You could proclaim "Thou shalt not kill!"
Fisher of souls, You went out in the morning
With a paltry net of salesman's talk,
Now two thousand years are nearly over
Show me, just how great has been Your haul?
Weak in spirit and slow on the uptake,
You believed in God and in the Tsar,
I shan't make the same mistakes as You did,
Not a single one of them I'll share!
All the world won't find a single scoffer
Who would lift a lance against my power,
If I die—one day it could just happen—
My kingdom will endure for evermore!"

Chapter 3: Night in the Moscow Suburbs

All alone, and feeling horrible,
His windows lost in the gloom,
He's counting his steps—there's more of them
Every time he crosses the room.
From corner to corner in stupor
Strides the clockwork automaton,
A hundred beds he could choose from,
But he can't get to sleep in one.
As he crosses the naked parquet,
At each pace he pauses to breathe,
He can't get rid of his headache
And that buzzing noise in his ears,—
As if someone had plucked a bass string
With a finger, then dropped from sight.

What is he to do in this waking,
What to do in this lonely night?

Get drunk on wine? Call the doctor in?
But the doctor's a killer, the wine's all piss . . .
The whole world's filled with sleep and joy,
But he must answer for everyone!

As if scrubbing away the pockmarks
He wipes the sweat from his face,
For what reason, why, O Lord God,
Has his been so cruel a fate?
Desertion, betrayal, desertion,
Have numbed the whole of his life.
"Why're you hiding behind the curtains?
Sergo, there's no need to hide!
I'd like your face to warm up
This dull, unwelcoming room,
Sergo, sing me something Georgian,
Old friend, my favorite tune,
Our forefathers' age-old ballad
As they set out on their last road,
Sing, Sergo, and forget that bullet,
For even ten minutes, forget!
Enough, that's enough, shut up, no more!
You base betrayer—away with you!
Away with them all—form up to rot!
And all their kin one hundred fold!"
Everywhere—ill will, foes on all sides,
Like a fever's chill he strides and strides . . .

Over grizzled capital cities
Night and darkness, too thick to see;
Lady presidents sleep with their presidents,
Kings lie sleeping, and ministers.
The world had thundered its marches
And slept, snow-wrapped from head to feet,
His ministers slept and his marshals . . .
He didn't know that they weren't asleep—
Lying low, the morning's orders
They awaited with fear and hope,
He felt worse all the time, such nausea,
And his boots seemed to fit too close . . .
Then unbidden, against regulations,

The church bells began to toll.
And he fell to his knees: "O Savior!"—
He said in a breaking voice,—

"Almighty Creator, to Thee I pray,
Send Thy quick messenger to my aid,
Oh give me, give me—not blood, but wine . . .
How does it go on? . . . But never mind,
Say not "No further, the end is nigh,"
Forgive me, Father, save me . . . forgive . . ."

Chapter 4: Conversation at Night in a Restaurant Car

Railway train and evening lights,
Long long road before us . . .
Come on, mate, let's have a bite
And a drop of vodka.
Bassan-bassan-bassana
Bassanata, bassanata . . .
Whether there's some wine or not—
Can't help feeling nasty.
I've gone grey before my time,
I've got one leg withered,
Ever heard of Magadan?
No? Then just you listen.
Let me tell you how it was:—
It was sort of night time,
Who should come into our hut?
—The Chief with all his sidekicks.
Thought this time they'd come for me,
Said goodbye, with cursing,
Chiefy had a cucumber,
Chewing on it thoughtful.
Took a bite between his words,
Ugly mug all spiteful,
"There's just been the top-rank court
Of our glorious Party,
They discussed the matter of
China and of Laos,
But a special point concerned
Our Paternal Genius."
Finished off his cucumber
And his speech in torture:

"It turns out our Father was
A bastard, not a father."
Well, that takes the bloody cake!
Requiem celebrations!
Orders—remove straightaway
His statue from the station.
Just imagine—storming snow,
Darkness, cold and icy,
There he stood in just a coat,
An ordinary private's,
Posed as if he's bursting through
Like a troop of cavalry.
Got my pickaxe to his boot,
But it wouldn't have any.
When I was a silly kid,
My old man related
He had helped to smash to bits
The church of Christ the Savior.
Bassan-bassan-bassana,
The devil with his oppo,
Bugger smashing up a church—
Just the people's opium—
But he's the Genius of all time!
There we stood, we cried and cried,
Guards and cons together.
They let rip with dynamite,
Put on final sanctions,
He fell down and so did I,
Blocked up half the station ...
Well, they crossed our time away,
Wrote us down in records,
And I'm still alive today,
Though you see I'm mental.
Bassan-bassan-bassana
Bassanata-bassanata!
Through the carriage windows fly
Baby Satans, baby Satans!
Keep your paws off, coffin meat!
Get to hell, God love us ...
Railway train and evening lights,
Long long road before us ...

5. A Chapter written while heavily under the influence, and constituting an authorial digression

Well, at least it keeps gossips happy,
Me, I'm not ashamed of being dim;
I can't be a Ptolemy (sorry!)
Even Engels, I can't match him.
But my rushing about in a lather,
Brought down that the world's amiss,
Tells me something's wrong in the setup,
And I ought to be getting to grips.
But this age has me gripped tightly,
It makes every initiative fade;
No prescription to cure this sadness,
All we had has been locked away.

But nevertheless, risking being thought
A clown, a fool, or a jester,
All day and all night I keep saying one thing—
No need to be frightened, people!
Don't be scared of jail or of going broke,
Don't be scared of plague or famine,
There's only one thing that you need to fear:
The man who says "I know the answers!"
Who says, "Come on, people, and follow me,
And I'll teach you all the answers!"

And pledging his troth to you all,
He'll pass over the earth like a ploughshare,
And drown the whole lot in blood.
He'll shoot such a load of humbug,
And weave such a cunning tale,
One that often enough in your camp hut
You'll recall in your hour of pain.
Blood's much less salty than tears,
It's give-away merchandise!
And History compels—Salomea
With the Baptist's head on a dish.

The earth is ashes and water tar,
There's no way to turn, so you're thinking!
Inscrutable are the devil's paths,
But no need to be frightened, people!
Don't be scared of ash, don't be scared of blame,

Fear not hell's fiery furnace,
There's only one thing that you need to fear—
The man who says "I have the answers."
Who says, "Every man that will follow me
Will get heaven on earth for his payment."

I elbow my way through the bar-room,
Go up to my bosom pals,
With the help of a little vodka
We have a heart-to-heart chat.
And my buddies look on sternly
To see I don't spill a drop,
"God's a friend of yours?" they say, smirking,
"No, I've not had the pleasure, by God."
I admit that a bar's not the best place
For a talk about evil and good,
But we've seen that "best of possibles,"
Yes, we've seen it all before.
It's cheap vodka for some and brandy for some,
Why the hell suck up to the bosses?
But I keep telling them, like a fool,
"No need to be frightened, fellows!
It's crazy to say there's no through road,
And you shouldn't come in without knocking;
The only person you have to fear
Is the one who says "I know the answers."
So drive him away! Do not trust in him!
He's lying! He has got no answers!

Chapter 6: Ave Maria

The case was a put-up job—anyone could see it,
But the questioning flogged into its second month:
The grim-faced interrogator on tranquilizers for breakfast,
A beard like a prophet's sprouting on the subject's face . . .

> . . . The Madonna walked on through Judea,
> In a garment blue-bruised by laundering,
> On she walked, a pack on her shoulders,
> With every step growing more lovely,
> With every sigh growing sadder,
> On her head a careless kerchief,
> Cynosure of all earthly suffering;

And downcast behind her shambled Joseph,
The Lord's stepfather, side-stepped by glory . . .
    Ave Maria . . .

They packed the prophet off to the Komi Republic,
He threw himself headlong in the weeds and grass,
The grim-faced interrogator got from the Party office
His perk—a month all found in Teberda . . .

  The Madonna walked on through Judea,
  On the sodden clay her feet were slipping,
  And the thorns were tearing at her garment;
  As She walked, of her Son she was thinking,
  And about her Son's fatal sufferings.
  Oh, how the Madonna's feet were aching,
  How she felt like sobbing like a baby;
  As she passed, the local flashy yobbos
  Let fly at her with horse-laughing comments . . .
    Ave Maria . . .

Later there exploded all sorts of cockinations,
The frowning investigator retired to Moscow, pensioned off;
A rehabilitation order with a seal upon it
Was posted to Kalinin to the dead prophet's wife . . .

  The Madonna walked through Judea . . .
  Ever lighter, ever slighter, thinner
  Grew her body with each step she took . . .
  All around Judea went on roaring
  With no wish to think about the fallen.
  But into that loam were laid down shadows,
  Shadows hid away in every footstep,
  Shades of all Butyrkas and Treblinkas,
  Betrayals, treacheries, and crucifixions . . .
    Ave Maria . . .

The Night Watch

When the town celebrations fade away,
The unrighteous and righteous in bed asleep,
Those the state has put by for a rainy day
Step down quietly from their pedestals.
In their hundreds of thousands, identical,
Along moonlit paths they go pacing,
And the odd belated pedestrians
Dive for shelter in first-aid stations.

      And drums are a-drumming!

Clock pendulums freeze, stand motionless,
The hands on their faces pull backwards,
A uniform statue with soldier's step
Marches out, repeated in thousands.
Some of marble, and some of brass made,
Some are holding that famous pipe,
Alabaster ones, shattered fragments,
Itch to follow, like white-flecked tide.

      And drums are a-drumming!

I lean out from my window, shivering
With a fever, one hundred Celsius,
As the brazen generalissimo
Heads a pageant of fools and jesters.
He climbs up on the hallowed podium,
"Of all peoples and ages the genius,"
And salutes a parade of monsters,
As he did in those days so dear to us.

      And drums are a-drumming!

By the wall of the block my flat's in,
Among heaps of abandoned dust and trash,
You can make out a goose-stepping jackboot,
And a broken-off piece of moustache.
For the moment, they creak, drop a curse or two,
Now, they only leave fading traces,

But the last little button's certain to
Come in useful again on occasion.

And the drums will be drumming!

Dawn's pink fingers suffuse our motherland,
Station callsigns ping down the radio waves,
The bronze statue returns to its place of rest,
Alabaster ones stay in their hideaways.
Maybe crippled, just temporarily,
But their fragments retain the makings,
Alabaster only needs humankind,
And again it will rise to greatness!

And the drums will be drumming! . . .

The Lady Beautiful

Song of the Lady Beautiful (A Woman's Waltz)

Can't believe that you are my wife,
Can't believe that you are alive!
For you see, I thought I'd simply
Created you in my mind.

Don't consider yourselves the guilty ones,
And searching to find your punishment;
And don't look at us with those furtive eyes,
Those eyes that have been over-terrified.
As if called by vocation and summonses
You grind down our agony with tolerance,
Makes no difference that you were born latterly,—
You know everything, know how to do everything!

Can't believe that you are my wife,
Can't believe that you are alive!
For you see, I thought I'd simply
Created you in my mind.

You've never known any dissembling,
Never cruised by Butyrka jail's windows,
And you've never spent rainy nights shivering
At the accursed gates of Lefortovo.
But winds are going to blow menacingly,
Your unshod feet will pace out calamity!
Makes no difference that you were born latterly,
You know everything, know how to do everything!

Can't believe that you are my wife,
Can't believe that you are alive!
For you see, I thought I'd simply
Created you in my mind.

Times have given us no glad inheritance,
We've been swamped in blood and baseness,
But with your magnificent helplessness
It's our pride, not our lives, that you've salvaged!
You won't reap your reward a hundredfold,
We'll tread separate paths through this century,
Makes no difference that your were born latterly,
It's never too late for militance!

103

I'm so scared that you are my wife!
I'm so scared that you are alive!
One night in Yaroslav prison
I created you in my mind...

Tonechka

She collected up her things, and she said delicately:
"So you've fallen for this Tonya—best of luck to her!
Don't pretend it's her wet lips have cast a spell on you—
It's because her daddy's got a lot of privilege;
He's got coppers on his gate, a nice place out of town,
Dad has pretty secretaries and smooth young men around;
Daddy's got a CC card to buy from closed foodstores,
Dad can go to private films, that don't get shown around.
But this Tonya girl of yours, she's really horrible,
(Take no notice what I say—I'm not important now!)
And you're going to sleep with her—flat as an ironing board,
Just because her daddy's got a government limousine ...

That's what you were out to get, you know it's true,
You know it's true, won't admit it though,
All this talk of love, all this talk of trust,
And such wonderful oh-so-noble stuff ...
When you've really got your eye on that place out of town,
Sentries and secretaries, and those smooth young men,
How you'll be sitting watching films with all the family,
And you'll roll it round your mouth just like a caramel."

Now I'm living in that house—I couldn't ask for more,
No more buttons to come loose—all my pants have zips,
And the wine they have in stock—as much as you can drink,
And the toilet here's as big as my old living room,
And we eat off china plates—enough to serve a king ...
And when daddy gets back home late in the evening,
All the guards and smooth execs have to watch their step,
And I serve her dad a shot of vodka on the rocks,
And I crack a little joke about the four-by-twos!
But when I get into bed with that stupid Tonechka
I can't help but think about another gentle voice,
Hard to get along with, though, she's just impossible,
When I call her on the phone she just hangs up on me ...

Driver, driver, take me to Ostankino,
Ostankino, you know, the Titan cinema,
That's where she's working now, she's an usherette,
Standing at the door cold and shivering;
Cold and shivering, frozen to the bone,
But she's overcome that old love of hers,

105

Rigid with the cold, frozen, growing old,
But she's not compromised, she's not forgiven me!

A Jolly Little Chat

Well, her mummy let her do what she wanted,
"My Red Riding Hood," she'd say, "little nestling,"
Brought her cocoa every day, two whole glasses,
For herself, a drop of tea—nothing extra.

Then one July day they buried her mummy,
Not a penny piece she left for her daughter;
But some kindly people came along to help her,
And she started on the till in a grocer's.

And she's sitting there at the cash-desk,
Just as if it's a public scaffold.

The till goes ting-ting-ting, the till goes ting-ting-ting,
Big Bad Wolf's gobbled Riding Hood,
And her dark-haired fringe is swinging,
The till goes ting, ting, ting,

What a jolly little chat!

Then the manager made eyes in her direction,
(Might be interesting to see what would happen!)
All he got was her reply from the cash-desk—
That she'd wait for Mister Right to appear.

Told them all where to get off,—one exception,
And she called this one "Alyosha, my sweetie";
And by trade he was a cash-desk repairman,
He was going bald, and Jewish—but decent.

Then wartime came along, he enlisted,
She cried the night away—and back to business.

The till goes ting-ting-ting, the till goes ting-ting-ting,
But his regiment got smashed to bits,
And her fringe of streaky hair's swinging,
The till goes ting, ting, ting.

What a jolly little chat . . .

Only yesterday, it seemed, she was twenty,
But her little girl was nine years old already,

And the manager still tried to get round her,
But he didn't stand the slightest of chances.

So he shopped her for no reason, just malice,
He regretted it, but couldn't reverse it,
They discovered that she'd got money missing,
And they pulled her in to face criminal charges.

Off she went to do time in camp and jail,
Then came amnesty, and back to the till.

The till goes ting-ting-ting, the till goes ting-ting-ting,
And its catches are wearing thin,
And her rusty-haired fringe is swinging,
The till goes ting, ting, ting,

What a jolly little chat!

But she loved her little girl, raised her carefully,
But before she could turn round—she was twenty!
Why on earth did she keep popping in the grocer's
And the manager—why was he always smiling?

Next July there was a lovely big wedding,
On the street where we all live things were humming,
And the kindly folk in front-doorstep gossip
Says the manager now calls her his old mummy.

At her cash-desk she's still sitting,
And her grandson's in the infants.

The till goes ting-ting-ting, the till goes ting-ting-ting,
In copecks measuring life's bill!
And her fringe of white hair's swinging,
The till goes ting, ting, ting,

What a jolly little chat...

Ballad about the General's Daughter

> "For he was a titular councillor,
> And she was a general's daughter..."

Made the bed and put some coal on the stove ...
And I chopped a bit of gherkin and meat;
In he came, stretched his legs, and lay down—
'Cos his fancy piece has got the painters in.

He's very glad she has, the pup, very glad,
Knocks his vodka back, he's dead to the world!
... And back in Russia, there's this town, Leningrad,
And there in Leningrad's the Boundary Canal.

Where my dad and my mum used to live,
Used to call me, they did, "sweetikins,"
And they loved little me such a lot,
But the both of 'em, they got the chop!

Oh Karaganda, oh Karaganda!
With your heaps of coal coming up the shaft!
Twenty years I gave, thirty years I gave,
My man's someone else's, haven't got my own!
Kara-gan-da ...

He's a boozy taxi-driver by trade,
He's a fence and a pimp, and he's tight,
There's no flies on him where money's concerned,
Gets a rouble or as much as he can!

Gave me a lift once to the grocery store,
Made a dead set at me, didn't mess about;
I'd have panicked, but I saw in the car,
He'd a postcard on the windscreen, the swine!

And on the postcard there—a city garden square,
And in front, the rock with the Bronze Horseman,
Now thirty years ago mummy took me there ...
I can't go on with this, I'll start to scream and shout!

Oh Karaganda, oh Karaganda!
Some you take to your heart, some you treat like dirt,
Far as I'm concerned, you've been so nice to me

That I'm no use at all to myself no more!
Kara-gan-da!

Then he wakes up and he lights a fag,
Picks his jacket up with wallet inside,
He slops off in his bare feet down the hall,
Then comes back and straightaway stretches out.

He lies snoring and I sit by the fire,
For the vodka chopping onion up fine,
After all, he's got some pity for me,
At least he's flesh and blood, damn his eyes!

Hushabye, just you sleep, my own treasure,
Tears, you know, never made bread taste better,
If his fancy piece is preening her feathers
Couldn't give a toss, I'm not your proud empress . . .

Oh Karaganda, oh Karaganda!
If you're proud round here, you're worse than no damn use,
And our daily bread give us, Lord, this day,
Back there in Russia they're no better off than us!
Kara-gan-da!

Just can't get to sleep, now I feel wide awake,
And tomorrow there's a hell of a lot to do!
They're supposed to bring us herrings from the store,
And I've heard it said that they're from Leningrad.

I'll buy some to keep and give a few away,
Best put something by for the holidays!
Half a dozen I'll send to his fancy piece,
Let her have some fun, something nice to eat!

Hope she has a feast, the poor old idiot,
Musn't let her think I'm a greedy one,
Now my eyes are stinging—it's the onions,
And somehow I can't keep my head up straight . . .

Oh, Karaganda, oh, Karaganda!
With your heaps of coal coming up the shaft!
But on the postcard was a city garden square,
And in front, the rock . . .
Ka-ra-gan-da!

In Memoriam

Gypsy Romance

A girl met up with a god.
The god was getting dead drunk in a bar-room,
Is there much to be gained from a god
In the devilish fumes of hard drinking?
Oh, how he drank towards midnight!
How his head was ringing,
And how those gypsies, the swine,
Were singing "Konavella"!

"Ay da Konavella, gran-tadella,
Ay da yorysaka palalkhovella!"

And the girl sat there with the god,
Faced the god, side on to the others;
She ought to run home to her daddy,
But she's clinking champagne glasses.
Oh, Christmas trees and bits of frieze,
How sweet the wines go down,
In a silver tassie
On a plate o'gold!

Raise a glass to whom? Here's a health to whom?!
To Crown Prince Alexandrovich!

The samovars' plating gone to hell,
Fug over the tables like new-turned earth,
When it got towards four, nearly morning,
The god chucked down his last hundred note . . .
Drunk to the wide, the god
Was tut-tutted by everyone,
Not a peep from the gypsies,
The gypsies had wandered off,
His friends had drained their glasses,
And gone upon their way!
The girl was the only one
Who hadn't deserted the god.

This girl lived by the river Okhta,
Her eyes were the color of ochre,
And mummy waited up for her treasure,

But she and the god were embracing.
The floorsweeper, turning his nose up,
Flicked his wet rag this way and that,
And the god, hanging his head,
Hunched his shoulders as if from the cold,
Asked the gypsies for even one word,
Even the tiniest one, even ever so soft,
But his answer—a bowl of salt water,
And "Past closing time, did you hear?"
Instead of vodka he got water,
Instead of beer he got bubbles,
Then the girl started
Delicately singing:

"Ay da Konavella, gran-tadella,
Ay da yorysaka palalkhovella ..."

How that girl sang to the god!
Sang of meadows and of journeys,
Sang of twilight and of dawnings,
And loved ones gone away to sea.
Oh, how that girl sang to the god!
Oh, how that girl sang to Blok!
And she didn't, she didn't know
She'd become immortal that morning.

That delicate voice in the fug of a bar-room
Will for ever ring out in the *Nightingale Garden.*

August Again

Anna Akhmatova in memoriam

Anna Akhmatova greatly feared August, she didn't
like it at all; she thought it her unlucky month, and
she had very good grounds, because it was in August
that Gumilev was shot at Berngartovka station, in
August her son Lev was arrested, and in August the
notorious decrees about the journals *The Star* and
Leningrad were published, and so on. "The Crosses"
is a Leningrad prison.

"There wasn't enough paper—please forgive me,
I'm writing on a manuscript of yours . . . "

Anna Akhmatova, *Poem without a Hero*

In ill-omened silence, deceptive
Shades of bridges with broken backs;
She would walk along the Shpalernaya,
At the Crosses she'd hang about.

Hard to bear, but then in some ways
Familiar as hand on pen,
If only it wasn't August,
The month of the devil himself!

That August of old had been just as
Deceptive and just as absurd,—
Through the black Berngartovka heavens
Calamity flashed like a bird.

And wouldn't it again be August
In a year that was yet untold—
Bovine roars condemning her writing,
And conscience bought and sold?

But that would be later; meanwhile
Yet another Leningrad night—
She'd given up hoping for miracles
If only she knew he's alive!

And clearly inked in the twilight
As it's inked into all our fates
Her regally careless forelock
Gummed down to her moist forehead.

The sigh of Finnish pinetrees,
Reward for all her work,
But again there's autumn coming—
Disaster time for you!

It's August, and it looks like
Things all as used to be,
A fat-faced Buddha lying
That grief's no tragedy!

A forelock curling, curling
In ringlets on forehead,
Young girl goes into darkness
To try what fate will send.

Along a street unlighted
With challenging patrols,
She walks in that immortal
Way you used to walk.

To festival and scaffold
She is going just like you,
Through Pryazhka and through Prague
To find Crosses of her own!

Let stupid neighbors gossip all they want to,
Let someone give a gentle reprimand,
She will return home as the day is dawning
With not a single word of where she's been . . .

She'll lick away the ink from sweating fingers,
And say, as she leans back against the wall:
"There wasn't enough paper, please forgive me,
I'm writing on a manuscript of yours . . ."

The Return to Ithaca

Osip Emilevich Mandelstam in memoriam

...in the Mandelstams' flat were Mandelstam him-
self, his wife, and Anna Akhmatova, who had come
from Leningrad to visit them. There they sat, all
together; and for the whole time the search was in
progress, in the next flat their neighbor, the poet
Kirsanov, who knew nothing about the search, was
having a party; the party also went on until
morning, and they kept on and on with records of
Hawaiian guitar music, which was fashionable at
that time...

And the only light
Is in star-hung, barbed-wire untruth,
But life will flash past
Like the foam of an actor's cape,
And there's no-one to speak
From the herd on the darkened street...

Mandelstam

Next door all night long a guitar went on twittering
As their neighbor cranked up his birthday, the boor;
Like ambulance men, the two peoples' witnesses,
Like ambulance men, the two peoples' witnesses
Yawning and pining by the dark door.

And those fat fingers with slow deliberation
Went on with their infernal occupation;
And in silence looked on the two sovereign ladies
As the fingers dug into the rough-textured papers,

They greasily leafed through one book then another;
The king, for his part, he sidled and strutted,
So his glance wouldn't betray which page was important,
And to blot out beside him those unseeing faces!

The fingers were seeking sedition, sedition,
Next door they just wouldn't stop playing "Ramona":
"Ramona, I hear the mission bells above,
Ramona, they're ringing out our song of love,"

"...But life will flash past
Like the foam of an actor's cape..."

He thought, as the fingers frisked the upholstery:
That freedom you used to have was so fine!
Now swallow the dregs of your Jacobinism!
Now swallow the dregs of your Jacobinism!
Not vinegar yet, but no longer wine,

You nutcracker-starling, you simpleton-Simon,
Why on earth did you mess with an alien triumph?!
On what have you squandered your golden bullion?!
The witnesses' eyes followed him in boredom ...

The ladies sat smoking, that's all they could think of;
Cursing, upbraiding themselves for the things
They'd not done, the careless nod at the station,
All the things there had never been time to tell him ...

The fingers kept digging, the paper was ripping,
The heartbroken tenor next door kept on singing—
"Ramona, you are my love, you are my dream,
Ramona, you'll always be the one for me ..."

" ... And the only light
Is in star-hung, barbed-wire untruth ..."

And down that black street, behind the "black raven,"
Behind that carriage with windows all barred,
I'll rush to and fro, ceremonial sentry,
I'll rush to and fro, ceremonial sentry,
Until I fall flat when my strength has ebbed!

But the word will survive, the word has survived!
The heart, not the word, is what becomes tired;
And want to or not, jump down from the whirligig,
And like it or not, the epic has finished!

To Ithaca we'll never cruise under canvas,
In our age the vehicle is prisoners' transport,
Odysseus packed off in a wagon for cattle,
Where the only good thing is they call off the trackers.

To cheer up his mates in the truck, full of moonshine
A thief from Odessa starts singing "Ramona":
"Ramona, just listen to the tender breeze,
Ramona, a wordless song for you and me ..."

"And there's no one to speak,
There is no one to speak!
From the herd on the darkened street . . ."

B. L. Pasternak in Memoriam

"The governing body of the USSR Literary Fund
announces the death of B. L. Pasternak, writer and
member of the Literary Fund, which took place on
30 May of this year, in his 71st year, after painful and
prolonged illness, and conveys condolences to the
family of the departed."

*The only announcement of the death of B. L.
Pasternak to appear in the newspapers (or rather, in
one of them, the* Literary Gazette).

They dismantled the wreaths to make yard-brooms,
For about half an hour wore long faces;
We contemporaries, we're so proud of it—
It was home in his bed he departed!

Third-rate fiddlers torturing Chopin's tune,
At the solemn progress of parting,
In Elabuga he didn't soap a noose,
In Suchan he didn't run ranting!

Even "penpashas" in from the provinces
Arrived in time for the party;
We contemporaries, we're so proud of it
It was home in his bed he departed!

It's not as if he'd just turned forty,
A good age to die—spot on seventy!
And he wasn't some adopted orphan—
Litfond member, the late lamented!

Those big hands of his sprinkled with evergreens,
His snowstorms have fallen silent . . .
And we're so proud, rotten nonentities,
It was home in his bed he departed!

> "A snowstorm raged o'er all the earth,
>   In every corner;
> The table bore a candle's flame,
>   A candle burning . . ."

> No! Not one candle there at all—
>   Electric light bulbs!

120

The executioner's spectacles
    Flashed fast and slyly!

The yawning audience all were bored
    As windbags ranted,
"T'aint jail or exile, after all,
    Or death by shooting!"

Condemned not to a crown of thorns,
    On the wheel harrowed,—
Instead, his face with cudgel scourged,
    To death by ballot!

Someone kept asking, in his cups,
    "What for? Who was he?"
And some were chewing, someone chuckled
    About a story . . .

That laughter we shall not forget,
    Nor yet the boredom!
We'll know each one of them by name
    Who did the voting!

"The murmur dies. On stage I've made my entrance.
And leaning on the framework of the door
I try to catch . . ."

Argument and slander silent fallen,
Eternity, it seemed, had granted us parole . . .
But above the coffin rise the looters
In a ceremonial patrol!

Whispered Cry

Warning

Warning

Don't you order liveries with gold braiding,—
You won't join in privy councils, sons of David!
Grieve ye not, on wailing waste not one minute,
For you'll never sit in senate or in synod.

You will sit instead in exile and in prison,
And they'll take away the laces from your shoes,
On the Sabbath you won't sing songs and praises,
You'll be hauled up for a grilling by the screws.

If you start to trade in soft soap and unction,
And you make yourself the sort of Jew that's useful,
They will let you call yourself "Russianante"
And award a star to pin on your skullcap.

If you prosper in soft soap till you're first man,
Never fear, you'll never join the inner circle;
Soft soap never made an Orpheus, sons of David . . .
So don't order liveries with gold braiding!

Dozing Off and Waking Up

January snowdust sprinkled everywhere,
And the drawn-out nights are fiercer now;
I am asking people for forgiveness
For the simple reason that it's done.

Sparrows find a shelter in the starlings' nests,
Starlings flown away beyond the seas;
Sinner, I ask sinners to forgive me,
This scoundrel calls on scoundrels to forgive.

Now my sabbath star is brightly burning,
To vengeance and to blame indifferent.
I shall now put on a change of linen,
On the table seven candles set.

Night will start to fall, and then the devilish
Jazz of wind and scouring snow begins . . .
I shall fall asleep, and dream of fragrances—
Snow and fire, and wet-through animal skins.

But then, surfacing from past times bottomless,
There will come a small voice pinched with cold—
I will hear Arina Rodionovna
Saying "*Nit gedeige!* Sleep, my son,

Disinfectant's rotted convict clothes away,
And our griefs have all been totted up,
And by Babii Yar—laughter, an orchestra,
All's in order, therefore. Sleep, my son.

Sleep, but in your fist clench tight your armament—
David's paltry armament—a sling!"
. . . People will forgive me from indifference,
Them, the indifferent, I shall not forgive!

Ballad of the Eternal Flame

To Lev Kopelev

...I've been told that the favorite tune of the commandants of Auschwitz, the tune to which they sent batch after batch of prisoners to their deaths, was "Tum-balalaika"; it was usually played by an orchestra of prisoners.
..."Crimson Poppies on Monte Cassino" is a song of the Polish Resistance.

"Unknown Warrior," wreathed in your military glory,
Are you dashing young hero or tragedy's seer?
Before this conundrum, with thundering drums rolling,
Heads of Government humbly are bending the knee.
Headstones stand like a shriek over graves without voices,
Headstones may not be essence, but simulacra,
Sometimes not to pain but the vain you're devoted,
Letters inset with gold upon slabs of black granite!

    Is all this tale told now?
    Pain gone for good, over?
    Trumpet in the ghetto, bidding
    All you dead men, battle!
    Trumpet, sing out, call out,
    Sing about my Poland,
    Sing about my mother,
    Thrown in a cess-pool there!
    Tum-bala, tum-bala, tum-balalaika,
    Tum-bala, tum-bala, tum-balalaika,
    Tumbalalaika, spiltbalalaika,
    Oh, my heart's aching and breaking in two!

Now the merchants arrive in Poznan,
Soap and furs are the goods they're buying,
While there's still time left for pausing
Don't forget what things were like then.
Scythed by fire from those black machine guns
In our final unseeing onslaught
"Blood-red poppies on Monte Cassino,"
We were falling among those poppies.
In the picturesque market, meanwhile,
Sometimes deutschmarks were rustling, then roubles,
"Blood-red poppies on Monte Cassino,"
Now you're black poppies for a funeral!

But the trumpet calls us to combat,
And commands us to go on struggling!
Sing to us of the world's most horrible,
Of the world's most stable currency!
Tumbala, tumbala, tumbalalaika,
Tumbala, tumbala, tumbalalaika,
Oh, my heart's aching and breaking in two!
You recall how a crazed young lad
Led his squad on the Appelplatz,
Tumbalalaika, spiltbalalaika,
In the gas chamber they dance the Totentanz...

Another thing:
Mazurka step,
A crouch and then a walk,
Two convict soldiers try to nab
An enemy who'll talk.
Mazurka walk, mazurka crouch,
And dyed moustachios,
A clock ticks in a soldier's pouch,
His trophy from the wars!
In Poznan three whole days and nights
We went out on the spree...
My mate escaped unrecognized,
But a patrol got me!
Oh, bright blue jewel of the dawn
And sunsets' aniline,
While soldiers' boots go marching on
Against Berlin city!
Profundo thunder rumbles on
Around the firing line,
My comrades' boots go marching on,
But I've been left behind!
Hard by a river's curving bend,
A resting place of green,
Where sleeps a soldier who's been trained
To fire a gun and kill!
The broad highway, the open road
Is my last bivouac,
I'm short of one thing I should own:
An epaulette with a star.

Don't you grieve for me, my own mother dear,
You sleep on peaceful, take your ease,

And fare thee well, recce company,
And Comrade Stalin, I must leave!
Don't you mourn for me, my own mother dear,
For fate is blind, as people say,
It might come to pass that the folk will keep
Weeds from sprouting where I'm laid . . .
And still more:
Where political prisoners roamed,
Searched their compounds for rotten roots in the snow,
Not one Premier on earth will confront this scene,
Hitch up his pants and go down on his knee!
By the Kama and Ob, in Siberia's wastes,
No wreaths and no flags will be laid on these graves!
Their eternal flame, their glory undimming
—Just the logpiles, the logpiles, that stand by the river!

Later, my friends, later
We'll put paid to pain for ever,
Trumpet, sing out, ring out!
Ring out, announce battle!
Brazen and full throated
Sing ye of my Potma!
Sing of my own brother
Laid in the cold northland!
Oh, how that brazen bitter blare
Calls you to combat, calls you to dare!
Tumbalalaika, spiltbalalaika,
This was the song as we went to our deaths!
Tumbala, tumbala, tumbalalaika,
Tumbala, tumbala, tumbalalaika,
Tumbalalaika, spiltbalalaika,
Oh, my heart's aching and breaking in two!

31 December 1968, Dubna

The Train

S. M. Mikhoels in memoriam

It's ages since we brandished
Either anger or reprimand;
We exchange "good-days" with bastards,
With quislings we shake hands.

We're not anxious to search or do battle,
All is just, everything's to our liking,
But remember—a train is departing!
You hear it? A train's departing
On this day and every other.

But we crack our jokes and pull people's legs,
The flattery of foes is like water from a well!
But somewhere over tracks, tracks, tracks—
Wheels, wheels, wheels, wheels . . .

We're of such peaceful disposition
That without any effort at all
We can call the shortest distance
The route that goes round about.

The polis has paid its insurance,
The queen is preparing dinner,
But remember—a train is departing,
You hear it? A train's departing
On this day and every other.

We'll polish the floor, hang up shutters,
So our heaven has no slant or limit.
But somewhere over tracks, tracks, tracks,
Wheels, wheels, wheels, wheels . . .

By the speed of our age made somnolent,
We live, not counted as living;
Non-resistance of the conscience—
Most convenient of eccentricities!

But once in a while, in the stomach
A knife-thrust, brooding and angry—
Our train is departing for Auschwitz,

130

That train of ours leaves for Auschwitz
On this day and every other!

Like our destinies, as if they were linked,
Uphill all together, derailed all together!
For all time over tracks, over hearts, over skin—
Wheels, wheels, wheels, wheels!

Kaddish

Kaddish is the Jewish prayer of remembrance, pronounced by the son in memory of his dead father. This poem is dedicated to the memory of the great Polish writer, doctor and pedagogue Jakow Goldschmidt (Janusz Korczak), who perished in the Treblinka death camp along with his charges from the Warsaw Orphans' Boarding School.

I'm so tired of repeating again and again the same thing,
Falling, returning again to the circles I've travelled before,
I do not know how to pray, O Lord my God, please forgive me,
I do not know how to pray, forgive me and come to my aid . . .

But every evening there's always the same music playing:

"Got the Saint Louis Blues, you scald and you hurt my soul,
Yes, those Saint Louis Blues, and the horn begins to choke!"

> But you just sit there listening
> With your eyes fixed fast on me,
> Your entrance paid, you're listening
> With your eyes fixed fast on me,
> You're chewing, drinking, listening,
> With your eyes fixed fast on me,
> But this horn of mine sings of a treetop
> The one where I'll string you up! Yes, suh!

"I bear malice towards no one; I don't know how, I simply don't know how it's done."

Janus Korczak, Diary

And out of Warsaw are departing trains,
The ghetto ever more empty and more dark,
A garret star looks through the window panes,
The trains hoot in farewell the whole night through,
And I bid farewell to my memory . . .

> The gypsy was a smooth-tongued thief,
>   And twice as sweet for that,
> He touched his seven singing strings,
>   Smiled at me, and he said:
> "My son, my son, you must take heed
>   Of gypsy reckoning—

God made the seven days of the week,
    The devil these seven strings,
And in this crafty reckoning
    There is a hidden sense;
Remember, even the rainbow is
    Also made up of seven
Colors..."

The brass of autumn time has singed the city,
Of all its wonders I am guardian,
A coin that can't be changed bestowed on me,
Twice seven years my age, and I'm in love
With all princesses and all girls who're plain;
O, cover me with thy extended wing,
My childhood's city with thy unnamed mysteries,
I'm glad that in disaster and festivity
Thy servant have I been, also thy king.
And I have tried to do all that I could,
Not once entreated fate for liberation!
Now I declare, as at extremest unction,
If there should be on earth a children's God:
Lord, I have received all things in full,
In what department must I make my statement,
One thing alone I ask—save me from hatred,
That is one debt that I have not incurred.

And now, a doctor in the year of war,
I—five times seven, this age—twice seven years old;
There's blood and sweat filling the ambulance train
Delirious, a man sings. I recall
His words, with sadness and with strangeness filled:
    "Shine on, shine on, O star of mine,
    O star of love, O star of welcoming,
    You are the only thing I'm cherishing,
    There'll be no other..."
There was such a calamity happened that day;
By a watery path through a forest,
To take leave forever of me, an alien,
You crossed over your country's border.
And could we have seen in that fateful year
This disaster would be a salvation?
Like an empty sleeve, a fading ensign
Fluttered over the planks of the platform.
An alien winter suddenly came;

It was somehow familiar, though alien,
In that tawdry cinema a French film played,
People bartered for Austrian remnants,
The cabbies geed up their broken-down nags.
In a cafe with shutters nailed tightly
We sat, you and I, drinking cognac
And eating a dried-up apple.
In silence, we knew things were finished for us,
From doomed hopes we sought no consolation,
And in silence we drank a toast to that star
That over a grave shone sadly:
            "If I should die, over my grave
            Shine on, gleam out, O star of mine . . ."
And out of Warsaw are departing trains,
It soon will be our turn, do what we may,—
But all the same, shine on, shine on, my star,
Shine on, shine on, O my six-pointed star,
Shine on upon my sleeve and on my breast!

A pet-name long forgotten, echo will respond,
The snow will spread out like a layer of gingerbread,
When I am once again a little babe,
The world again be big and festive,
When I am once again a heavenly cloud,
When I am once again a chaffinch bird,
When I am once again a little babe,
The snow once more will smell of apple fruit,
They'll carry me down porch steps, slumbering,
And I'll be woken up by creak of sledge,
When I am once again a little babe,
I'll find again a world of miracles.
Star in the window, star upon my breast,
No knowing which of them the brighter one,
But I am tired; and true, with hidden sense
The trains hoot in farewell the whole night through,
And I bid farewell to my memory . . .

In the Orphanage there also lived a little girl called Natya. Severe illness had left her unable to walk, but she was good at drawing, and she used to make up songs—here's one of them:

Natya's Song about the Little Boat

I have made a little boat
    Out of colored paper,
Out of clover, out of bark,
    On its flag a clover.
My boat's green and my boat's pink,
    Drops of resin on it,
,My boat's clover, my boat's birch,
    Little boat so bonny.
When the springtime waters start to run and gurgle,
    On a long, long journey over ocean blue,
Little boat will sail away to Salvation Island,
    There—no war, no shooting, all is peace and sun.
While I made my little boat,
    I sang like the chaffinch,
But I spent my time for nought,
    For my boat has perished.
Not in storm or lightning flash,
    Or thunder or whirlwind—
When the soldiers came to search
    They crushed it with their jackboots...
But when springtime waters start to run and gurgle,
    In the clouds a welcoming trumpet-call of cranes,
To the shore of sunshine, to Salvation Island,
    It is surely certain someone's boat will sail!

———————

At some time to come, when you are remembering the names of the heroes, please do not forget—I beg you, do not forget Peter Zalewski, ex-grenadier, war veteran, who worked as a watchman at the Orphanage and was murdered there by Polish quislings in the autumn of 1942.

Our modest yard he was sweeping
    That time when they arrived,
The conversation then was strange
    Like at the edge of the earth,
Like conversation at that bourne
    Where there's only "yes" and "no";
They said to him: "Hey you, hey you,
    Look sharp, come over here!"
And then they asked: "You are a Pole?"—

135

He answered—"I'm a Pole."
And then they asked how it was so,
    And he replied: "Just so."
"You want to stay alive, peg-leg,
    So why the bloody hell
D'you haunt the ghetto, like a Yid,
    With all the Yiddish kids?
Now why?"—they said, and on and on,
    "Why are you so stuck up?
We're telling you, Poland's out there!"
    But he replied: "It's here!
Poland is here and Poland's there,
    The same in every place—
Unhappy country that is mine,
    My beautiful country."
Once more they asked: "So you're a Pole?"
    He answered: "I'm a Pole."
"Well then," they said, "That's how it is";
    He answered them—"That's how."
"Well then," they said, "Enough of this!"
    They gave the order: "Fire!"
And before his body fell
    His crutches hit the ground,
Before he found eternal peace
    And sleep, and quietness,
To those who watched from the window
    He managed to wave his hand.
May God grant me an end like that,
    The cup of agony drained,
To those who watch from the window
    Manage a wave of hand!

———

And later there came the day when the Orphanage with its children and staff were ordered to report with their belongings at the Umschlagplatz (the name the Germans gave to the square by the Gdansk station).

The train is leaving on the stroke of midnight,
The idiot locomotive puffs "Shalom!"
Formed up along the platforms stood the blackguards,
The blackguards come to see the trainload off.
The train is leaving on the stroke of midnight,
The train is leaving straight for paradise,

136

How the blackguards dream that very shortly
They'll report that Poland's "Judenfrei."
"Judenfrei" are Warsaw, Poznan, Cracow;
The whole protectorate from line to line
Satanically black with spider markings
For now and evermore is "Judenfrei"!
On the Umschlagplatz close by the station
The ghetto waits exhausted—who'll be next,
Like a last hosannah thunder-quaking
Quisling's yelp: "The Orphanage is next!"
As the lips of the translator tremble,
Throats are dry and hearts gripped in alarm,
But old Korczak's on his feet already
Holding little Natya in his arms.
The standard bearer with his peaked cap turning,
His topknot curled as if it had been rolled,
And upon the banner green is burning
A clover leaf, a clover leaf of gold.
And the pair of buglers raise their bugles,
Standard bearer hoists his staff up straight,
Wind-kissed lips, the lips of little children
Start to sing a fearsome, jaunty song:

"Our glorious campaign's getting off to an easy beginning,
From the old city center to Gdansk bridge we're going,
And onward, and singing, formed up by our ages
Towards Warsaw's limits, by Gdansk bridge we're marching,
Along streets of Gdansk, along streets of Gdansk,
Step out our young girls, there's Marisa and Daska,
But little young Bolya, red-haired little Bolya
In shock he's got stuck at the edge of the water,
                              the edge of the water..."

You can smell the sea, it's warm and salty,
Eternal sea and mankind's vanity,
And upon the banner green is burning
The clover leaf, the golden clover leaf!
Lined up three abreast we now are filing
Down the ranks of SS carrion crows...
Further on, beginning of a fable,
As onto the platform out we go.
The interpreter runs up behind me,
Taps me on the shoulder timidly,
"Korczak, you are authorized to stay here,"

If the legend's true, I don't reply.
I take the children, as if through a lesson
To the train, this iron ferry-boat,
We should be walking out along the platform—
Along it, but we're walking straight across.
As we go, our patched-up shoes are rattling,
Straight across we go, and not along,
And the sniggering collaborators
Raise their leathered hands in a salute.
Weeping fades inside the hellish coaches,
And above the bustle of farewell—
There upon the banner green is burning
A clover leaf, a clover leaf of gold.
It could be that reality was different,
But *this* legend doesn't lie to you—
Out towards its final railway carriage,
Out towards its purgatory-carriage,
Out towards its chloride-scented carriage
Goes the House of Orphans with a song:

"Along the Lodz highways, along the Lodz highways,
Stride guests who've been loaded with all sorts of honors,
With little boys striding and little girls striding,
They puff at their whistles and twirl their rattles . . .
The streets and the trails and the high roads all lead us
To snowclad Zakopane, to blue-mountained Tatra,
And on the white summit there flies a green banner,
Beneath us the whole of our coppery Poland,
All Poland . . ."

———————

And at this point someone couldn't stand it any longer and gave the signal to start—and the Warsaw-Treblinka train, long before the appointed hour (a completely improbable event), set out on its journey . . .

Now the song is finished.
And the chatter is silenced.
Now the heavens in spasms
Book-bound in grilled windows.
For the land in his power
To the rattle of carriages
The king is inventing
A calm-making fable . . .
Let us begin, thanks being given . . .

138

"A hundred years ago,
In his court a sloppy prince
All over heaped up so much filth
He made himself quite sad.
One day he flew into a fit
And called his painter in.
"Has the time come"—so spake the prince
"To put some paint over this filth?"

The painter said: "It's time,
It's long been time, O high-born prince
For ages it's been time."
And filthy white became the filth,
And filthy blue became the filth,
And filthy gold became the filth,
Under the painter's brush.
And all because filth will be filth,
Whatever paint you use."

No, it certainly wasn't the time for this fable!
And my wonderkingdom didn't applaud it.
Unexpectedly then came the voice of young Natya,
Inappropriate too, saying "Goodbye, Warsaw!"
And then, like a beater on a length of railway,
Hearts started banging like a beater on a length of railway,
Hearts began sirening: "We'll come back to Warsaw!
We'll come back, we'll come back, we'll come back to Warsaw!
It spread through the coaches like forest fire,
From carriage to carriage, from one train to another,
It boomed out like an oath: "We will come back to Warsaw!
We'll come back, we'll come back, we will come back to Warsaw!
Though we melt into smoke over hell's fiery funace,
Though our bodies are turned into burning lava,
Still, as rain, still, as grass, still, as wind, still, as ashes,
We'll come back, we'll come back, we will come back to Warsaw!"

————

But I, what am I to do?
Anyway my heart's in tatters,
I shake in that very carriage,
I burn in that very furnace,
But from the year nineteen-seventy

139

I cry out to you: "*Pan* Korczak!
Do not return!
You will be frightened in *this* Warsaw!
The earth has been white-laundered,
There aren't any mounds or ditches,
There are obelisks of granite,
Insisting on deathless glory,
But tears and blood are forgotten.
Do understand this, Korczak,
And do not return,
You'll be ashamed in this Warsaw!
Bread and circuses granted,
Vistula annexed, and Tatra,
Earth, sea, sky—all are ours,
People say—but are they?

Thread of day in the autumn,
Weird call of the cuckoo,
Yours? Not true, they are *not* yours—
It's Kosciusko's autumn!
Sky with soot and dust laden
From the smoke of industry,
Yours? Not true, it is *not* yours—
It's the sky of Tuwim!
Stately sentinels, pinetrees
By the foam of the Baltic,
Yours? Not true, they are *not* yours—
They're the pinetrees of Chopin!

Tragedies gaily multiply,
Joy is convulsed in tears,
But have we seen much of joyfulness
In this our little sphere?

Do not return to Warsaw,
I am beseeching you, Korczak,
Do not return,
You have nothing to do in *this* Warsaw!

Homunculi strut like peacocks,
Twitch of heroic muzzles,
A rabble of gabbling garbage
Scrambles for unclean power . . .

140

Do not return to Warsaw,
I'm pleading with you, Korczak!
You'll be an alien stranger
In this, your native Warsaw!

———————

But every evening the music plays on and on, as if nothing had happened:

"Got the Saint Louis Blues, you scald and hurt my soul,
Yes, those Saint Louis Blues, and the horn begins to choke!"
  And on discs in mono and stereo—
  Declarations of burning love,
  And my horn's song is of a treetop
  Back in Saint Louis, my home town.
  In the land of my fathers, shooting
  In the dusty night, rat-tat-tat!
  Misters, get on with money-grubbing,
  To pay for your booze and your tarts!
  There remains—comical, isn't it—
  Just one little thing you owe—
  Lay out your remaining money
  To pay for this trumpet's song!
  But you just sit there listening
  With your eyes fixed fast on me,
  You buy your ticket and listen,
  With your eyes fixed fast on me,
  You're munching, drinking, listening,
  With your eyes fixed fast on me,
  But this horn of mine sings of a treetop
  The one where I'll string you up! Yes, suh!

———————

I'm so tired of repeating again and again the same thing,
Falling, returning again to the circles I've travelled before,
I do not know how to pray, O Lord my God, please forgive me,
I do not know how to pray, forgive me and come to my aid . . .

Goldminers' Waltz

Goldminers' Waltz

We've called ourselves adults for ages now,
We don't try to pretend we're still young,
We've given up digging for treasure trove
Far away in the storybook sun.
We don't make for Equator or polar frost,
Or get the hell off out of sight;
It's silence, not treasure, that's gold for us,
And that's what we dig for, all right.

Hold your tongue, and you'll make a bomb,
Hold your tongue, hold your tongue, hold your tongue!

For years we hardened our minds and hearts,
It was wiser to keep your eyes low,
Many times, many ways we played silent parts,
But that silence meant yes, and not no!
The loudmouths and moaners who caused a fuss,
Not one of them's lived to grow old ...
It's the say-nothings now who rule over us,
Because, you know, silence is gold.

Hold your tongue, you'll make number one!
Hold your tongue, hold your tongue, hold your tongue!

And now we've survived to see better things,
Everybody keeps talking a lot,
But behind the bright jewels of rhetoric
That old dumbness spreads out like a blot.
Someone else can lament about violence,
About hunger and insults untold!
We know there's more profit in silence,
Yes, *we* know that silence is gold!

It's so easy, making a bomb,
It's so easy to make number one,
Or to have someone shot for a song:
Hold your tongue, hold your tongue, hold your tongue!

Waltz Dedicated to the Regulations for Guard Duty

Generation of the accursed!
Only recently, so long ago,
We had fun with our giggling girlfriends,
And we packed every cinema show.

'41 came along, blowing icy,
And we suddenly had to grow wise;
We were drilled in the science of sciences
By a bastard in corporal's stripes.

Oh, that coarse-woven joy, regulations—
Even sleeping, don't ever forget
That a move in a rightwards direction
Begins with a step by the left.

And then in our bright medal ribbons
We puffed out our chests and walked tall,
We got married to any old scrubber
Just to make up for time we had lost.

We strode over Red Square in triumph,
Full of glory, the men of the hour;
On the podium He stood there smiling,
With his bodyguards throwing flowers.

Oh, our marching steps rang so blithely,
We so easily wrote off our debts;
We forgot that a move to the right must
Always start with a step to the left.

What's become of your courage, you skivers,
Was this really the dream in your eyes?
Those deserters got going with their trials,
It was then the fur started to fly.

"Answer, soldier boy, what's eating you up?
Answer, soldier boy, what's eating you up?
Answer, soldier boy, what's eating you up?
Soldier, soldier, let's have less of that crap!
Fought your way, you say, from Volga to Vistula,
And you didn't look for rank or easy number?

You're not dead—why not? I want to know the reason,
By the figures, you should be six feet under!"

What the soldier said could barely be heard,
What the soldier said could barely be heard,
What the soldier said could barely be heard,
"I just happened not to die, 'scuse me, sir!
Please forgive me for not catching a bullet,
Looks as if those bullets hadn't eyes to see, sir,
Just like medals for political merit,
There just didn't seem to be one for me, sir!"

"Let's have less old soldiers' yarns, soldier boy!
Let's have less old soldiers' yarns, soldier boy!
Let's have less old soldiers' yarns, soldier boy!
You're a citizen, and it's pity you want?
You've no money, and no flat for your family?
And the kind of thing we're after's unknown here?
You're the only loyal man in this factory?
And the others are a load of old scroungers?"

The deserter-procurator raves and rants,
The deserter-procurator raves and rants,
The deserter-procurator raves and rants,
And his sentence is—ten years in the camps!
Oh, my friends, you poor suffering idiots,
Back again to the slime of new roads;
But those barbed-wire frontiers and limits
They have taught us a lesson of gold:

Don't go sparing a crust for a scrounger,
Don't let flattery lead you astray,
Don't believe in a sky blue and cloudless,
Or the smile on a fat shining face.
Maybe fame has come back now to pet us,
And our enemies call themselves friends,
But a move to the right,—we'll remember,—
Always starts with a step by the left.

To the Congress of Historians

Blood washed half the kingdom, the times out of joint,
And then it was said with a vengeance:
"Prince Oleg the Wizard prepares to go forth,
On the turbulent Khazars wreak vengeance."

    These words that resounded like clamoring brass,
    All of us used them, and more than just once.

But an eminent man in the course of a speech
Once declaimed with fine enthusiasm:
"The traitor Oleg once cooked up an idea
To wreak vengeance on our brother Khazars."

    Some words disappear, other words make the pace,
    One truth then another assumes pride of place.

So remember, you people, know once and for all;
And be damned to all stupid confusion:
"Some sort of Oleg took revenge for some cause
On some Khazars for some sort of reason."

    This legend comes down from the hoary old past—
    Instructing historians in our native land!

---

*In his concerts after he left the USSR, Galich prefaced this song by saying:
"This is my proposed speech at a proposed congress of historians from the
Socialist countries, if such a congress should ever take place, and if I were ever
granted the high honor of giving the introductory remarks." But he replaced
the final couplet with a new conclusion:*

    And this Marxist approach to olden times
    Has long been applied in this country of ours.
    It's come in very useful in this country of ours,
    And it'll come in very useful in yours too,
    Because you're in the same . . . camp;
    You'll find it very useful.

*I am very grateful to Vladimir Frumkin for this text, which has not been
published in Russian.*

Untitled

To V. Benyash

Even my time for grey hairs has come,
I can hear the carrion crows,
"Judge not, that ye be not judged . . ."
So the counsel of nonsense goes.

Ah, that ice-cold gulp of oblivion,
It readily makes me see
That extravagant hero Budenny
Gallop on his extravagant steed.

So come then, my friends, let's treble
The gold reserve of our power,
"If you don't touch us, then we won't . . ."
It's a song we've sung over and over!

Judge not!
          And meeker than Abel,
For a roof and a crust bow low;
So there was some writer called Babel
And he's gone—that's how it goes!

Judge not!
          And there's no yardstick,
Words excepted, anything goes;
Some Marina or other choking
In a noose—that's how it goes!

Judge not!
          Daub your gorgeous sunsets,
Get on playing your dominoes;
So what, if some loon in a compound
Screams of Phèdre?—that's how it goes!

"And I shall never see the famous Phèdre
In an ancient many-circled theater . . ."

. . . No, he won't ever see the famous Phèdre
In an ancient many-circled theater!—

146

From the depths of my misty blackness
I appeal to the historian—
From your store of abounding wisdom
Grant me even the tiniest portion!

I seek not the path of schism,
I'm prepared to walk straight and narrow!
Comfort me, I who have no comfort,
Enlighten, for I have no clarity!

"There is no other country that I know
Where so freely . . ."

Off you go then, get on with voting,
In closed ranks drill and march about;
The chosen will do the judging,
Unauthorized persons keep out!

With a speed that can't be imagined
Passing time has greyed my temples,
"Judge ye not, that ye be not judged . . ."
So one really shouldn't judge?!

So it's right to slumber soundly,
Drop your coin in the subway toll?
And judging, ordaining—why should we?!
"If you don't touch us, then we wo . . ."

No, this formula for existence
Is despicable through and through!
It's the chosen alone can be judges?!—
I'm not chosen, but I shall judge!

We're No Worse than Horace

Oh, you're all insufferably on the ball,
When the chips are down you're all such paragons,
Getting all uptight about your preview dates,
Making sure you never miss a show's first night.

All your furious ravings in an undertone,
Coddled by the guardian angel censorship!
But if there's nothing brand new on the scene,
There's your comfy little flats on new estates.

Where the wise old jailers never smile on you,
With their beaming blessings full of sanctity;
Just a little picture on the windowledge,
It's sufficient, you've no need for more than that.
Just a picture standing on the windowledge,
There's no need for more than that.

You've cast out your conscience and your fearlessness,
Just as if they couldn't be pawned and then redeemed,
Oh, you swinging idiots, exhibitionists,
Hands in pockets making V-signs—very bold!

Please don't let me stop you saying fiction's fact,
Daring to name names among your guardians;
But among you swinging monsters' grimacings,
There are wandering parasitic chroniclers.

No one coos their names on stage in honeyed tones,
And they're never graven on a dustjacket;
Just four copies knocked out on a typewriter,
And that's all, but there's no need for more than that.
Maybe up to now four copies' all there are,
There's no need for more than that.

History sows the winds and hurls down thunderbolts,
Sets up highpowered councils, boards advisory,
Every day the trumpetings of wordlessness
Sing the praises of profound stupidity.

Untruth ranges round her far-flung territories,
With her neighboring Untruth pools experience,

But the still, small voice of song comes thundering out,
And the bellow of the whispered undertone.

There's no hall, no red-plush auditorium,
And no swooning claque to clap uproariously,
Just an ordinary tape recorder, but
It's sufficient, there's no need for more than that.

Right, one picture standing on the windowledge;
Right, four copies tapped out on the typewriter;
Right, a single ordinary tape machine;
There's no need for more than that.

The Law of Nature (After Béranger)

Hup-two, left-right,
Three-four, left-right,
Hup-two-three,
Left, two-three!

On night watch went the company
All at the king's command,
Drum-major leads the company,
Tra-la-la-la-la-la!
Hey, citizens! Lock up your wives,
And don't get taken by surprise!
Drum-major leads the company,
Tra-la-la-la!
Maybe cowardly in action,
Not a penny to his name,
Never mind, he's very handsome,
Damn it all, so very handsome!
And he looks so very brave!

Hup-two, left-right,
Three-four, left-right,
Hup-two-three,
By the left, two-three!

The stars shine on the company,
Earth trembles 'neath their tramp,
They march onto the Devil's Bridge
Tra-la-la-la-la-la!
Precise of step, by starlight lit,
They strode onto the Devil's Bridge;
It gave a lurch and cracked to bits!
Tra-la-la-la!
As if swallowed by some creature
They all sank beneath the waves,
For there is a law of nature,
Yes, there is a law of nature,
Alternation is its name!

Hup-two, left-right,
Three-four, left-right,
Hup-two-three,
By the left, two-three!

150

The throne has long since gone to auction,
The king is long since dead,
But that law is still in action,
Tra-la-la-la-la-la!
And if that law's not in your head,
You'd better get it in your head,
That law is one you can't reject,
Tra-la-la-la!
Keep repeating in all weathers
Not for its impressive sound,
But believe it, you had better:
If you keep in step together
Then the bridge will tumble down!

    Hup-two, left-right,
    Three-four, left-right,
    Hup-two-three,
    By the left, by the right—
    Break step!

The Ducks are Flying

To L. Pinsky

From the north, from the island of Zhestev,
Ducks on the wing,
Six of them, six of them, six of them,
Grey ducklings,
Six of them, six of them, flying south . . .

No more furrowed brows, no more unpleasantness!
Let's stop raking up things of the past!
But whenever I suffer from sleeplessness
Once again there comes to my mind—

Curdled sunset falls
Across the taiga,
And five hundred cons
Formed up in the snow,

Soaking rain was whipping its sponge about,
Building up and then dying away,
And the screw stood there with his Alsatian
And I'll tell you the speech he cracked at them:

"Dog, damn it all, never never does
Eat, damn it all, his fellow dog,
But if anyone gets out of line,
He'll be eating snow!
And I'd like, damn it all, to remind you,
That a single step to the side
Will be, damn it all, deemed to be
An attempt, damn it all, at escape!"

The arctic blizzard's running mad—
Doesn't look who it strikes,
But five of them, five of them, five of them
Still flying on,
Five of them, five of them, flying south . . .

But then maybe it really is shameful
To say the same thing word for word,
But whenever I suffer from sleeplessness,
Once again there comes to my mind—

152

Standing straight, not huddling,
Cons in the snow,
They're discussing creation's ways
In the Central Comm.

Photographers' lenses flashing
Ugly mugs smell of shaving cream,
And the armed guard stood spit and polished
Not looking like a screw:

"Dog, beg your pardon, never does
Eat, beg your pardon, his fellow dog!
But have all of you taken to your hearts
The teachings of So-and-so?

And I'd like, beg your pardon, to remind you,
That a single step to the side
Will, beg your pardon, be deemed to be
As, beg your pardon, flight!"

A shot, and aimed from above the wind,
Bullet hits heart,
But four of them, four of them, four of them
Still fly on! . . .

And if even one of them flies all the way, and even if
noone flies all the way, all the same, it was worth it,
it was necessary to fly! . . .

Fame is the Spur

"In the night there comes . . ."

In the night there comes a black raven,
To my sleeplessness the pathfinder.
Even if I strain my voice, wailing,
I can never make my wail louder.

You can hardly hear at five paces,
People warn me even that's crazy.
But the point is, it's by heaven's grace that
People hear at even five paces!

The Transmigration of Souls

Please, no cutting capers when I go,
I'm not hoping for the joys hereafter;
I'd prefer that my immortal soul
Pass into some sneaking rotten bastard!

May the swine dissemble and betray,
May the crow be taken for a falcon,
May no fatal bullet chance his way,
O'er his path may stormclouds never gather.

Always with his finger in the pie,
Cradled by companionship and comfort,
Numbered with the elect by those on high,
Sticking pins in other people's numbers.

May he prosper as the time goes by,
Day by day—but then, all of a sudden,
With a rush, may this despair of mine
Clamp its black paw on the bastard's gullet!

A Song about Tbilisi

The gloom of night envelops Georgia's hills . . .
Pushkin

I failed to understand you once before,
When you were wrapped up in the mists of winter;
You fled the gaze of people not your own,
But you still had a beauty unalloyed,
And, poisoned by my grudges, I was guilty.

And it was you beside me at the feast,
When wakefulness went on into the morning;
With reeling head I plunged in Kura's stream;
How could I possibly next day have seen
In my hostess' eyes contemptuous boredom?

Around me in a ring there tightly snapped
The ebb and flow of your unceasing clamor.
And every time your bitter wine I sipped,
Wherever faded wallpaper had slipped
I always saw the whiskered face of Stalin.

When next I came, your native flute conversed,
Once more, his glass in hand, with rage and fury
This worthless poseur gabbed his stupid stuff . . .
And I was almost charmed by your rebuff,
And by your twisted smile that meant no hurting.

And in the aeroplane as I flew home,
I looked with shamefaced pleasure at the Georgians
To Moscow still embraced by winter's cold
Transporting bright persimmon by the load
And baskets of the earliest mimosa.

I didn't see; it never crossed my mind
How great a triumph you were celebrating,
How big a lesson you had taught my pride,
When, stumbling, I had circled far and wide
Along a false trail laid deliberately!

Persimmon, Stalin, all these things you have,
The fug of feasting, morning light on churches;
You keep these things to keep from going mad.

Your inner essence is a thing apart,
It only comes at times of its own choosing.

And at these times, false trails all fade away,
And wounds begin to heal beneath the bandage;
And, shining on the slopes of Mtatsminda,
A haughty voice of happines and pain,—
The deathless voice of Nina Chavchavadze!

A country full of beauty and of pride!
To words of evil, jokes your only statement;
But suddenly your flute becomes a cry,
And every single drop of bitter wine
With a sweet aftertaste of blood is tainted!

When ragged mists beyond the river float,
And forecasters predict a day's bad weather,
I see the parchment burning into smoke!
I hear the roar of lorries and their horns!
I hear the boots of convoy soldiers treading!

Your peace is trampled by those soldiers' nails!
Your women cannot sleep, your children calling,
The thunder of those boots the country fills!
But you accept your misery like guilt,
As if alone you're answerable for all things!

These fist-clenched ashes do not lose their heat,
And memory still wears its stone-chilled clothing,
And still, a striking dagger from behind ...
"The gloom of night envelops Georgia's hills ..."
And there is still so far to go till morning!

The Old Prince

Same old whirligig—lodgings and cities,
Smell of greasepaint, wigs full of dirt, . . .
Like an old man-o'-war hit amidships
I'm adrift far away from my berth.

I've steered clear of the mines till this last one,
And it seems like the very first time,
That the signalman means what he taps out—
Hopeless Morse that spells SOS.

Growing old is a cruel little number,
You can't shrug it off like a coat,
I'm an old man-of-war going under,
And it seems as if nobody knows.

Voices sound all around, dictating,
On the walls there's a blur of old bills,
And out there queuing up in patience
Are the folk who still trust in me.

Many roads, many lodgings I've been in,
Many beds with revolting sheets,
And I've banished all sorts of Ophelias
To their nunneries with no release.

Now the courtiers back off, bowing, scraping,
Spilling powder from made-up gray hair,
All the extras go off, but I'm staying
Face to face with the audience, alone.

On my own! No one else in the action,
And the fate of this drama's all mine;
The young girls and lads in the gallery
Can't help holding their breath for a time.

I'm an old man who suffers from asthma,
Standing bracketed by the spots,
And a faded old bouquet of asters
Has been left on my table top.

So many kind, unloved people
Have witnessed my flops and my hits

I stand nonplussed, not hearing
What comes from the prompter's lips.

But my failing body's laughed at
By a shudder that goes right through,
And the word once again becomes action
That can turn the world upside down.

Shakespeare's text is put by and forgotten,
I don't want to remember my lines,
Like a voice from a world misbegotten
I cry out with only my lips:

THE TIMES
        ARE OUT OF JOINT . . .

An icy hand runs down my body
And my clenched fist trembles aloft,
And the audience hiss to each other:
"That line's not in Shakespeare, he's wrong!"

But the gods won't hold it against me,
They know why I speak out of turn;
But the man-o-war's bulwarks crumple,
And the sea floods over the stern.

My Friends Keep Going Away

To Frida Vigdorova

> On the back page of the paper they print announcements of deaths, and on the front page—
> theoretical articles.

They're leaving, they're leaving, they're leaving,—my friends;
Some on their way down, others in the ascent,
They leave in the fall and they leave in the spring,
As if every day were the first in the week,
They're leaving, they're leaving, they're leaving,
My friends are going away.

Don't come running round to tell me a secret:
For I won't believe it, I just won't believe it,
Then first thing next day along comes the paper,
And the paper gives my loss confirmation.

If one only knew in time who to watch for,
And for whom your smile's the last that will bless them,
On the back page—those who won't be returning,
Always less than those you find on the cover.

They're leaving, they're leaving, they're leaving, my friends,
Some into the bag, others to the attack.
The wind that is raging in this age of ours,
It cuts down your friends and it spares not your foes,
They're leaving, they're leaving, they're leaving,
My friends are going away.

We all used to dream such dreams of ocean fastness,
Think we'd make it straight to some tropic island!
Like a bugler boy in shock after battle,
I send out a call to friends still surviving.

And I call the roll by taste and by touching,
Count them off, but then again in the morning,
Once again there comes the paper with its summons
That I'm duty bound by grief to respond to.

They're leaving, they're leaving, they're leaving, my friends,
They're leaving like cavalry into the mist,

160

They don't care for rights, conscience is but a fig,
Some don't give a damn, but then some will forgive!
They're leaving, they're leaving, they're leaving,
My friends are going away.

Since the thunder of one loss then another's
Rolled around the hearts of all on this planet,
Don't come running round to try and console me,
Telling me I'm not the only one suffering.

Don't you proffer me returns on disaster
Like a handful of small change in worn nickel!
For I don't intend to mourn the departed—
I can't tell who's dead and who is still living.

They're leaving, they're leaving, they're leaving, my friends,
Some on their way down, others in the ascent,
They leave in the fall and they leave in the spring,
As if every day were the first in the week,
They're leaving, they're leaving, they're leaving,
My friends are going away . . .

"A clapped-out professor of history . . ."

A clapped-out professor of history
Will start writing at some time to come,
And there will be comical misery
In his leisurely tale about us.

He'll write it with insight and feeling,
Eliminate faults as he goes;
It'll all be arranged nice and neatly,
And everyone stripped to the bone.

And straightaway, right in the middle,
That insolent bone will stick out,
The butt that a guest, drunk and fuddled,
Leaves stuck in the food on his plate.

Now what, you might say, could be simpler
Than to throw it away and forget?
But the wine of oblivion won't rinse out
Those ashes that stick in your throat.

And the bones that come next will be smaller,
Compared with the big one that sticks,
But strangely resembling each other
In their scurrilous nudity.

A pencil-end, soap-stub, old footwear
That others have used up and leave—
A footnote—no more than a footnote,
Will be all that historian spares me.

For the sake of this one little mention,
A pathetic few droplets of ink,
I've constructed my own isolation
And hoisted my cross on my back.

So just for one little mention,
A contemptuous tip left by time,
For this I once said farewell to
The world with a generous smile,

Put premature years on my loved ones,
And strode past the pale with my songs,

Made people who loved me tearful,
And left them to weep alone.

But things I have said in a whisper
Will ring out until Judgement Day,
So what does it matter if history
Won't grant me the foot of one page!

15 January 1972

Petersburg Romance

To N. Riazantseva

"There's no cause to pity him,
...He himself is to blame for all his regrettable
disasters,
For he tolerated things that a man cannot tolerate
without becoming contemptible ..."

N. Karamzin

... Really, I should feel calmer,
Not just seem so, but be!
... But these bridges, like chargers
Every night, up they rear!

Here those regiments ever
Form a square in the dawn
Stretched from Synod to Senate
Like four lines of a poem!

Here, in vapors of liquor,
In the setting sun's flame,
There has been so much witchcraft,
So much covertly whispered;
There has been so much witchcraft,
So much covertly whispered—
Just try doing it again!

All the griefs of the earth have
Shown their face in this place ...
Now we're paying with silence
For the part we have played!

... These boys with their beardless faces
Just subalterns were, mere ensigns;
These boys must have been quite crazy,
The last thing they need's my counsel!

They ought to be taking the waters,
Away at the spas and seaside;
Instead in the night they cry: "Patria!"
And: "Tyrants! The dawn of freedom!"

No subaltern I, but a colonel,
I've fought, stood my ground in battle;
I thought these young pups were merely
A rabble of childish prattlers.

I too have denounced dictators,
And liberty I have lauded;
Our fire-eating declamations
Were washed down with wine like water.

And then came that fateful morning;
It seemed not at all disgraceful,
So wise it seemed, so discerning,
To say that one wasn't available.

Oh why, then, should it have happened
That the glow of my famous story
Should dim like a moldering ha'penny
In the sun of their rising glory?

Worsening weather, wounds start aching,
The years go by, grey and cheerless;
But I did, I did curse dictators
And lauded the dawn of freedom!

Whisper's chain is unsevered,
We retrace others' steps—
But foreknowledge has never
Saved one man from his end,

For how long, for how long, Lord
Not just here—everywhere
Will those desperate horses
Still submit to the rein?

Things don't get more straightforward,
Our age puts us on trial—
There's the square—will you go out,
There's the square—dare you go out,
There's the square—will you go out,
There's the square—dare you go out
When the right time arrives?

Where the squares of the regiments
Wait the signal to go,
Stretched from Synod to Senate
Like four lines of a poem?!

22 August 1968

Hussar Song

Copying a peasant artist,
Someone sewed into a rug
Alexander Polezhaev,
Caped in black and mounted up.

My dark envy and my namesake,
Both our hearts inflamed by grief!
Secret envy, envy fatal
—Any doctor would agree.

Up and at 'em, up and at 'em, forward, men of the chasseurs!
Forward, brother officers, darlings of the Tsar you serve!
Oh, those shakoes and those capes, heroes one and all;
But whose heart were you pointed at, you pride of gunsmith's art?
Could it be this heart of mine, you pride of gunsmith's art?

After midnight came disaster,—
Not a bullet in the brain—
An imposing carriage started
Out on its nocturnal way.

Nothing for the road, no singing,
No time for a glass of wine;
Three men go, I in the middle,
With a gendarme left and right.

Up and at 'em, up and at 'em, forward, men of the chasseurs!
Forward, men of the chasseurs, darlings of the Tsar you serve!
Oh those shakoes and those capes, it's time to make your show;
But this kind of arithmetic no poet will ever know,
In times gone by and times to be, no poet will ever know.

Where's your friends and all your fellows,
No one's here to save your skin!
Just a little song began it,
Then the thing got into print!

Down a razor's edge of torture
Slide, decide which way you'll go,—
Either all the way for poetry
Or straight to the mental home . . .

Up and at 'em, up and at 'em, forward, men of the chasseurs!
Forward, men of the chasseurs, darlings of the Tsar you serve!
Oh those shakoes and those capes, let rhetoric ring out!
But either way surveillance is much worse than shrapnel shot,
Denouncing and surveillance is much worse than shrapnel shot!

> Copying a peasant artist,
> Someone picked out in a rug
> Alexander Polezhaev,
> Caped in black and mounted up.

> Artist, drop your noble manner,
> Don't make heroes of our breed;
> Fate has handed us no banner—
> Just a bloodstained handkerchief . . .

Up and at 'em, up and at 'em, forward, men of the chasseurs!
Forward, men of the chasseurs, darlings of the Tsar you serve!
Oh those shakoes and those capes, holy standard's gleam;
It makes no difference who you're born, the century's a dream,
The century, the century, it doesn't mean a thing . . .

In His Image and Likeness

—or, to quote the inscription over the gates of
Buchenwald: *Jedem das Seine*—"To Each His Own"

One more day under way with its everyday cares,
That damned Mass that I'm writing has kept me awake,
There's a pain in my gut and a pain in my side,
And the house stinks as usual of washing and drying . . .
    "Morning to you, Bach," says God,
    "Morning to you, God," says Bach,
       "Good morning . . ."

But the first thing we hear when we rise from our beds,
    Just like crows shrieking down upon carrion,
The loudspeakers blare out, the loudspeakers blare out:
    "Up you get, good morning, dear comrades!"

And then, half asleep, we all get on the tube,
    Or the train or the bus or the tramcar,
Those loudspeakers keep bawling away, fit to burst,
    About triumphs and valor they clamor.

When I'm still half asleep there are times when I could
    In a fit of desperate violence
Smash those speakers, rip them down where they're hung,
    And bask in the beauty of silence . . .

Just you try it yourself, with your wife on your back,
To modulate through from X sharp to Y flat,
What with family rows and the money you owe,
There's nowhere to turn and nothing will go,
    "Keep your chin up, Bach," says God,
    "Have it your way, God," says Bach,
    "Have it your way . . ."

My gran's in a huff, and the wife's feeling bad,
    We're short of one thing then another,
I need medicine, I need a hospital bed,
    Can't see how in hell I can get it,

In my lunch hour I'm called to the Party bureau,
    The boss there, he hops and he dances;

"Well, if things are like that, we'll give you a sub,
    We'll slip you ten roubles for nothing."

The cashier spit-fingers the notes one by one,
    Meanwhile smirking a smirk like a robber;
I'll buy vodka (a half), and some sedative drops,
    And some cheese, and a chunk of best sausage ...

There's a cutting wind that says winter is nigh,
In St. Thomas' Chapel the door lets in draughts,
And the organ sings that the sum of all things
Is eternal sleep, corruption and ash!
    "Less blaspheming, Bach," says God,
    "Hear me out, please, God," says Bach,
    "Hear me out, please ..."

But that tart next door's got a booze-up on,
    Howling girlies and jackals chuckling;
I'll open my vodka and slice up my cheese,
    Give the missus her drops on some sugar,

And I'll pour number one, and I'll pour number two,
    I'll partake of my cheese and my sausage.
When the radio says I'm the salt of the earth,
    I'll hear with the greatest of pleasure.

And I'll stoke up my pipe that I brought from the war,
    Have a laugh at my carping granny,
And I'll pour yet again, and then yet once more,
    And pop round to the tart's for a fillup ...

He takes off his camisole, hauls off his wig,
In the nursery kids hiss—"The old man's back!"
Old?—He's past forty, a solid span,
The grey hairs like dust flecked around his lips ...
    "Goodnight, Bach," says God,
    "Goodnight, God," says Bach,
        "Goodnight ..."

A Song about the Ultimate Truth

To Yu. O. Dombrovsky

I'm successful, I sleep nice and softly,
In the future I won't have to sweat.
Trouble is, there's this place Missalonghi,
And I know that's where I will meet death,
I know that's where I'll meet my death!

In that place, driven crazy by travel,
With my pride and my status eclipsed,
Like Lord Byron, from truths in their thousands
I'll believe that the truth doesn't exist,
I'll believe that the truth doesn't exist!

And the weather that day will be lousy,
Sky and ocean will fuse into one;
And my friend, an informer and scoundrel,
Will poison the wine in my cup,
He will poison the wine in my cup!

My eyes will glaze over with mica,
And my notebook will fall on my knee,
And I'll say: "With a fever like I've got,
Why on earth did I have to come here?!
Why on earth did I have to come here?!

I shall see, as death's agony takes me,
That truth's neither here nor there;—
I, who dreamed every moment God gave me
Of my rightness I couldn't bear,
Of my rightness I couldn't bear!

But my friend, after dutiful weeping,
Will move into a dignified style,
Make a note in his diary: "Fever."
God forgive him, the poor man was right!
God forgive him, the poor man was right!

Fame is the Spur

" ...What can be heard of your songs, O Russia?
The Chud' have cast spells, the Merya have measured
Your log-paved paths, your roads, your milestones..."

A. Blok

I'm no priest of high culture,
I'm debarred from the shrine,
My song goes with supper
And a skinful of wine.
At the brink of disaster
Should I panic?—Begone!
If you'll pour me a starter,
I'll give you a song.
I will put on a show now,
Sing of Wonder and Fame,
But of shame I'll say nothing,
For I'm quite unashamed.
I'll just bend my soft backbone,
And I'll heap up your plate,
With much more than just backbite—
I serve civic complaint!

"How's life treating you, my sweeties?"
"Can't complain, can't complain!"

...Step inside now, gents and ladies,
(Help me, O thou righteous God!)
There'll be songs, and they'll be tasty,
Like meat pasties, piping hot.
And I've savories, salt and pepper,
Useful when you're feeling tight,
There's a girl with eyes of emerald,
Just the kind I've always liked!
Down the hatch with my first glassful,
Pour one more for later on,
And for openers, something special,
Here's my latest, brand new song:

"That's my mate's bed on the right, mine's the other,
Every other day we both have X-ray treatment,
Him, he used to be a screw, I a number,

172

Isn't it funny that it's here we should meet up!
And the two of us go strolling in the garden,
While I smoke a fag, he stands there and watches,
And we kid that hairy doctor, beg your pardon,
But we're feeling just terrific, Comrade Doctor!
So I stroll for half an hour with my old warder,
When we're tired we take a rest by the border,
And we strolled like this back there in the prison,
And I felt terrific then, can't say I didn't!
That's my mate's bed on the right, mine's the other..."

      Then a bunch of latecomers
      Interrupt my last verse,
      They get packed in the corners,
      There's no room left to turn.
      We don't notice their faces,
      Just we two in the crowd,
      So we'll pour out a chaser
      And we'll drink it right down!
      Oh, potatoes in jackets,
      Dear old Russia, my life!
      I'm ashamed... just a fraction,
      No I'm not, that's a lie.
      I'll stand up for my right to
      This low part that I play,
      To my cheap notoriety
      And my usual pain!

      "Got enough to eat, my sweeties?"
      "Feasting, feasting, feasting!"

      Sleighbells ringing, jingle-jangle,
      Drunken loutishness and row,
      Who would try to disentangle
      Plaintiffs from offenders now?
      They all look like plaintiffs, don't they,
      Punished by one God above,
      All anointed with one ointment,
      Some for wounds, and some for bugs!
      Fair enough then, knock it back then,
      But let's have a bit of peace,
      Please pipe down, you noisy bastards,
      So as I can say my piece:

"That's my mate's bed on the right, mine's the other,
And outside the snowstorm rages and thunders,
Him, he used to be a screw, I a number,
Now we can't get by without one another.
We're both pensioners these days, no more labor,
And our beds stand there like boats moored in harbor,
And beneath them on the shiny wooden parquet
Sit our slippers, just like two pairs of kippers.
And we talk of various things that we know now,
Like this clinic and the people who run it,
We compare sarcomas, they run the show now,
We two'd like to die both at the same minute.
Then one night, when all was quiet in the clinic,
My old warder propped himself up on his elbow:
"You were slippery, you were sly, you politicals,
What a fool I must have been not to nail you!"
He fell back and started gagging and wailing,
I'm afraid he'd had his lot, my old jailer,
And his bed sailed away to infinity,
Where the sentences are never remitted!
So I pulled the sheet up over my ex-warder...
Over Moscow it kept snowing and snowing,
And my son, arm in arm with his daughter
Through that very same snowstorm was strolling..."

My guitar strums a coda
As my voice softly dims,
Silence reigns for a moment
Because that's the done thing.
Pickled cucumber slices
Help the vodka go down,
"Now that song was a nice one,
This old feller's no clown!
That song hit where it ought to,
Don't forget how it goes,
Must remember the daughter
Getting led through the snow!..."
Unfamiliar faces
Drown in drunken despair,
And my sense of disgrace is
Like a punch in the head!...

"Informing all in order, sweeties?"
"In order, in order, by order!"

174

All the world floats round in circles,
Say hello and cheerio,
Everything is such a worthless
(Beg your pardon) puppet show!
Semi-halfwits on the payroll,
Such a lot of sweet young things,
Everything is just a gay old
(Beg your pardon)—whirligig!

...Here I sit, a poor performer,
Chuckle, rumble, chortle, roar...
And the next-door state informer
Hides his tape deck in its drawer...

When I return . . .

At Serebriany Bor, by the gates of the country club for actors of the Bolshoi Theater, there stands a wooden pillar, sunk into the earth and roughly squared up. Someone using a housepainter's brush and working carelessly and crudely has marked some divisions on the pillar and numbered them off from one to seven. On the top of the pillar is a little wheel, with a fairly thick string passing over it. On one side of the pillar the string disappears into the earth, and on the other a heavy weight has been attached.

The watchman explained it to me in the following way. "This here thing, Alexander Arkadievich, is what you call a shitometer ... the string, you see, goes down into the cess pit, so when the level rises, the weight goes down .... While it's around two and three, there's no problem ... but when it gets up around five or six, then there's trouble, you have to call in the night-soil men from town ..."

This achievement of Russian know-how seemed to me not only useful, but also instructive in the highest degree. So I dedicated a philosophical study to it, entitling it with epic restraint:

Landscape

All was grey and clouded over,
The woods standing as if dead;
Just the weight of the shitometer
Very gently nods its head.
In this world not all's in vain
(Though it mayn't be worth two bits!)
Just so long as there are weights
So you can *see* the level of the shit.

An Attempt at Nostalgia

...When they were driving across the Neva,
Pushkin asked jokingly:
"You're sure you're not taking me to the fortress?"
"No," replied Danzas, "It's just that the shortest way
to Chornaya Rechka goes past there."

*Taken down by V. A. Zhukovsky from the words of
Danzas, Pushkin's second.*

...It was last February time,
    Every so often
The table bore a candle's flame...

Boris Pasternak

...Pussy cat, keep away, an owl's
Embroidered on the pillow.

Anna Akhmatova

I regret not a thing, I regret not one thing in the slightest,
Neither frontiers nor years have dominion over my heart!
So then why should I fly into panic at just the idea
That I'll never again, that I'll never, no, never, oh God...
Just a moment, calm down, try and think—
If it's never—what then?

Arctic latitudes and their snowstorms,
Tarkhany, Vladimir, Irpen,—
So much that we never got down to,
Too late, surely, for cursing ourselves?

Our strength's ebbing more every moment,
Although our guilt isn't guilt.
Over system-built Russia the moon's out—
Number patch on a prisoner's suit.

And all those government buildings
Blood-blistered by snow and rain.
Blind-eye cataracts at their windows—
(For ages alone and friendless)
Faceless faces of leaders of men.

180

These wolves in their smoke-filled chambers
Lash at people as if they were dogs;
Then these wolves reach the end of their labors,
Into black limousines they clamber,
And light their imported fags.

These stars of the artisan quarters
Hole up in their state-owned retreats,
And gun-toting ugly-mug warders
Will see that they can't be seen.

And then in a stoked-up sauna
These hirsute tribesmen will jig . . .
You're not sorry for these things, surely?
Not sorry at all, not one bit! . . .

And I swear that I'll never remember the years of my childhood,
The coast at Sebastopol—infancy's shifting truth . . .
That mysterious hill where the Chersonese slopes to a quarry,
The descant of Hellas' dust on a child's sailor suit!
I swear I'll forget! . . .
But what won't I forget? . . .

What won't I forget? That repulsive
Sarcastic bureaucrat's face,
The clumsiness of my hurrying,
My final pathetic rage.

I've no faith in sighing for birch trees,
You shouldn't weigh partings in tears,
And where should this debit be charted,
Is the debit side where it should be?

We stand like a petrified forest,
Struck dumb, we wait on that shore
Where the body seems not to be body,
And words are not deeds any longer,
They're not even words any more!

Left behind by the generations,
Who dismiss us as they pass;
Derision, derision, derision,
Handed us like a new gift of vision,
Passport to our future at grass!

181

But the horses? Those winged horses
That strain from their stone pedestals,
The hunters whistling like outlaws,
The miniature bells of the sleighs?

Yuletide holidays? Fringe of a headscarf
Falling warm on a woman's breast?
You're not sorry to leave these things, are you?
Not very ... Well, maybe a bit!

But the candle of February's melting,
But owls on the pillow sleep,
But there's still the Chornaya Rechka,
But there's still the Chornaya Rechka,
But there's still the Chornaya Rechka,
Don't talk about that, shut up!

A Conjuration of Good and Evil

In this window the morning light breaks everyday,
Like a blind man, I know everything here by touch . . .
I am leaving this house, I am leaving this house,
I am leaving this house that doesn't exist!

It's a house and it isn't, it's smoke without fire,
It's a dusty mirage or it's Fata Morgana.
And jackbooted Good with the butt of his pistol
Used to rap on my door, keeping me under guard.

And cavalier Evil would wander beside me,
He'd repulse all attempts at breaking and entering,
And the saucepan and coffee-pot there on the gasring
Just got on with their jobs without playing the fool!

All entangled were Evil, Indifference, Good,
In a Moscow apartment the song of a cricket,
A whole year of grace in this world without gladness,
What man would deny things were going my way?

I can sing what I want, I can shout what I want,
I go clothed in this grace like a fitted-out beggar . . .
Never mind if these clothes made my gait a bit awkward—
I chose them myself for myself, to my size.

But the reason for Good's being Good, need I say,
Is to know how to feign being good and courageous,
To deem black to be white when the circumstance favors,
And to turn into silver the blithe mercury.

All is privy to Good, all is under Good's rule,
But don't look for a lot from this noble hero,
I could gladly run from him without glancing backward,
And dig myself deep into any bolthole! . . .

First to yield was the coffee-pot, bursting to bits,
Flooding the gasrings and making foul odors . . .
Up came Good in his thundering jackboots and shouted
That cavalier Evil's to blame for it all!

Next morning Good's agent came round to our door,
He was wearing (I fancied!) the cape of a policeman . . .

Just try running from *that* without glancing backward,
Find a bolthole to flee to from *that,* just you try! . . .

And this Agent informed us, deferential but stern,
That OVIR deals with questions of leaving the country,
That to live in our flat Evil hadn't a permit,
And one day was sufficient for packing our bags! . . .

So goodbye, my dear Evil, good Evil of mine,
Scalding candlewax spatters the lines of the psalter.
A whole year of grace in this world without gladness,
What man would deny things were going my way?

So farewell and forgive! The grain's swollen ripe,
The shipwrights are fixing the tar-coated planking,
And it's tears and not wax on the lines of the psalter,
In our glasses there sparkles the wine of farewell.

I have tended this cornfield for two thousand years,
Isn't it time I was hastening to bring in the harvest?
Don't be sad, for it's only for ever I'm going—
Leaving Good and this house—that doesn't exist! . . .

Odessa Memories

So you've learned how to play the fiddle then?
Saw that gut!
Plain-clothes Syoma yells "Thanks a million!"
Sounds like "Shoot!"

Syoma's out on the town with his lady friend,
Drunk and pleased.
This here lady, what do we make of her?
She's no peach!

Dark blue ribbon on ginger ponytail,
Awffly chic!
All the same, in David Oistrakh's company
I'm just nix!

But when Oistrakh plays it would never do
To drink cheap wine,
In this world everything is relative—
Einstein's right.

What we get in this life's on tenterhooks—
Joy and pain.
A sharp and *B* flat are fundamentally
Just the same.

There's so much that's been made and overmade,
Overspill!
And so much has been known and overknown,
Heaven and hell!

...So come on then, Lyubov Davydovna,
Off you go then, Lyubov Davydovna,
It's your solo, Lyubov Davydovna,
One—zwie-drei!
Smells and sadness filling the speakeasy,
Heart, perish!
One good thing, it's not like the West, where come

Midnight—sssshh!
Midnight means you can snatch a snort or two,
Oh, my Lord!
Get your patents off, haul on your outside shoes,
And—off home!

. . . I'm on my way home. I'm very tired and I want to
Sleep, they say that when at night people
Dream they're flying, it means that
They're growing. I'm not young, but
Almost every night I
Dream I'm flying.

. . . My dragonfly wings so lightly
Are trembling in winds that pass,
The green wedges of the pine trees
Beneath me rustle like grass.

And on to—Thalassa, Thalassa,
Creation's enchanted stay,
I'm only a ten-year-old lad now
But I really do know how to fly!

It's no fairy tale, I'm flying really,
Through the mists before dawning day,
Over boats with their varied rigging
And the city that's always grey,

Over dusty omnibus depots—
To the land that lives evermore,
Where again the Achaean elders
Make ready their vessels for war.

Another man's senseless grieving
Bids them bend their oars against Troy,
But I must beyond the Aegean,
I still have further to grow.

I'll grow to be brave and virile,
I'll accept the world like a prize,
And a girl in a dark blue ribbon
Will nestle up to my side,

Once more in the ruins of Ilium
The trumpet will call Helen's name,
And once more . . .

At the corner of Sadovaya Street three men stopped me. They knocked my hat off. Laughing, they asked: "Haven't you gone to Israel yet, you old git?" "What d'you mean, what d'you mean? I'm at home, I'm at home—so far. I still fly in my sleep. I'm still growing."

"Cough Your Throat Clear, February . . . "

Cough your throat clear, February, blast your blizzards,
Let your frosts crack down, unleashed from their traces,
We've been prodigal with our prometheanism,
Primogeniture we've passed unsuspecting!

Let's console ourselves with hospital wards, then,
And the way we never could make our minds up,
We've so gorged ourselves on dishwater pottage,
That we've never managed yet to get our breath back!

Listening to Bach

To Mstislav Rostropovich

My guitar on the wall started sounding,
And the wallpaper flowers flared.
Isolation that God's gift imposes—
So lovely, and so hard to bear!

In this world what could be more lovely—
(It spites all the plagues of this life!)
Isolation of sound and color,
The fall of a final line?

And fancy sets out on its journey
To the point where it becomes fact . . .
Who would dare to command the Lord God
And seek to control His paths?

The words that a verse line sculpted,
The canvas transformed into mist—
It's so easy to stretch and touch them,
The temptation's so hard to resist!

Lordly hangmen have no comprehension
That not all kinds of closeness are close,
The D minor Toccata's a temple,
And their permits won't open its doors!

Auguries of Spring

We would get together winter evenings,
Say the things we'd said the day before,
And from time to time there were occasions
When I felt that I could take no more!

We discussed inductions in close detail,
Made simplicity become complex.
My Calamity gave sidelong glances
At me—and beyond, at emptiness.

And, perplexed by these peculiar glances
(Tender looks that resurrected me),
Duped by my successes, I so often
Plighted my troth to Calamity!

Winter wouldn't pass, no signs of thawing,
Winter tried to conquer her heart's pain,
Home to Moscow I would rush from Tallin,
Out into the countryside again . . .

Red-lead undercoat painted the heavens,
April herded in a white snowstorm;
Suddenly, my ear tuned to the evening,
I heard the first patterings of the thaw!

It was the spring—the holiest of holies—
Bursting suddenly out of her bonds,
And the simple secret of communion
I discerned in the melting of snow.

When, as if mantled in mist, the waters
Started rising up above their banks,
My Calamity made me an offering—
An icon of the Virgin of Kazan.

The house was quiet, with a malty savor,
A pinetree gently creaked by the window,
Spring was saturated with the flavor
Of almost an autumn's singing gold!

This was spring of farewell and forgiving,
It was also my autumnal spring,
Teasing me with agonies of promise,
Taking sleep away, enervating.

... Seemingly before a distant journey,
Or perceiving dawn within the dark,
Thy holy gift with outstretched palm I'm touching
And pronouncing words confessional:
"At the threshold of a new Migration,
Now and evermore, eternally,
I accept with pride this my salvation
From Thy hands, O my Calamity!"

When I return

When I return...
Don't start laughing—when I return,
Over February snow, feet not touching the ground, I will hurry
By a barely discernible track to the warmth of a lodging,
To your bird-like call with a tremor of joy I will turn,
When I return...
Oh, when I return!

Do listen, do listen,
No laughing—when I return,
Direct from the station, curtly brushing aside the customs,
Direct from the station I'll burst my way into that city,
Infernal, despicable, artless, my bond and my hurt,
When I return!...

And when I return, I will go to a house that's unique,
Whose sky-blue cupola admits no heavenly rival,
Like the savor of orphanage bread, the savor of incense
Will strike into me and within my heart start to churn,
When I return...
Oh, when I return!

And when I return, though it's February nightingales will sing
That old melody, quaint and forgotten, sung into tatters,
And I will fall down, the conquered of my own conquest,
And buffet my head on your knees like a boat at the quay!
When I return...

But when will I return?!

Afterword to When I Return

That's all!

Sergei Eisenstein used to tell his pupils that they should shoot every single frame of their films as if it was the last frame they'd ever shoot in their lives. I don't know how appropriate this commandment is for the filmmaker's art, but for poetry it's a law.

Every single poem, every line, and even more every book is the last one. It follows that this is my last book.

Although at the bottom of my heart I hope all the same that I'll manage to write something more.

Paris, 10 April 1977
Alexander Galich

Notes

p. 59   *Ostankino:* a north-west suburb of Moscow.

p. 59   *Sheremetevo:* one of the Moscow international airports.

p. 60   *CC CPSU:* Central Committee of the Communist Party of the Soviet Union.

p. 68   *Advanced Party School:* an institute of higher education where candidates for posts in the upper echelons of the Communist Party are given specialist training.

p. 86   *Hospital Gypsy Song:* the title uses the word "gypsy" to refer to the mood and motif of the song, not its content.

p. 88   *The Error:* the incident that lies behind this song—the hunt traversing ground where the Red Army fought its bitterest battles—is said to have occurred when Fidel Castro visited the USSR at the invitation of Nikita Khrushchev, and the two leaders went hunting.

p. 90   *Stalin:* the epigraph is the last line of Alexander Blok's poem *The Twelve*; Jesus Christ is seen to be at the head of a detachment of Red Guards as they patrol revolutionary Petrograd.

p. 93   *Sergo:* G. K. Ordzhonikidze (1886-1937), an Old Bolshevik, a close supporter of Stalin and a fellow Georgian; in his secret speech to the 20th Party Congess, Khrushchev alleged that Stalin had forced Ordzhonikidze to commit suicide.

p. 94   *bassan-bassan-bassana:* the equivalent of "tra-la-la" in Russian gypsy song, to the most common *motif* of which this section was sung by Galich.

p. 94   *Magadan:* a region in the north-east corner of the USSR, one of the major components of the "Gulag archipelago."

p. 94   *top-rank court:* the reference is to Khrushchev's secret speech of 1956, which contained the first official criticism of Stalin.

p. 95   *The church of Christ the Savior:* an ancient church in central Moscow; it was dynamited before the war, but the building intended to replace it was never commenced; the site is now occupied by an open-air swimming pool.

p. 98   *the Komi Republic* is situated in the northeast corner of European Russia; it contains the Pechora region, one of the major components of the Gulag archepalago.

p. 98   *Kalinin:* formerly Tver, is a small provincial town to the northwest of Moscow.

p. 101   *The Lady Beautiful:* the phrase refers to a collection of lyric poems by Alexander Blok (1880-1921), inspired by a vision of divine feminine beauty and wisdom.

p. 103   *Butyrka, Lefortovo:* the two biggest Moscow prisons.

p. 104   *Yaroslav prison:* a notorious prison near Moscow, used as the main transit prison for offenders on their way to Siberia.

p. 105   *CC:* Central Committee (of the Communist Party of the Soviet Union).

p. 105   *Ostankino:* see above, note to p. 59.

p. 109   *Karaganda:* a region of Kazakhstan in Soviet Central Asia; its coal mines are an important part of the GULAG. The woman into whose mouth this song is put has been exiled to the region as a child because of the "crimes" of her parents.

p. 113   *Gypsy Romance:* dedicated to Alexander Blok. *Nightingale Garden* (p. 114) is the title of a cycle of lyrics by Blok dating from 1915. Certain periods of Blok's work are characterized by the use of gypsy and urban low-life themes.

p. 113   *river Okhta:* a small river that flows into the Neva on the edge of nineteenth-century Petersburg.

p. 115   *August Again:* the dedicatee is the poet Anna Akhmatova (1889-1966). The epigraph mentions the execution of her first husband, the poet Nikolai Gumilev, for alleged participation in a monarchist plot in 1921. The son of Akhmatova and Gumilev served several terms of imprisonment during and after the 1930s. In August 1946, the Leningrad literary journals *The Star* and *Leningrad* were singled out for special condemnation in the Party campaign to re-impose ideological controls in literature and the arts; Akhmatova, a contributor to these journals, was personally vilified and dismissed from the Union of Writers. Akhmatova was rehabilitated in the 1950s; from about this time she lived mainly at the writers' village Komarovo, on the Gulf of Finland outside Leningrad (p. 116, "The sigh of Finnish pinetrees/Reward for all her work.")

The subtext of Galich's song refers, of course, to the events of August 1968; "Praga," the Russian name for the city of Prague, is also the name of a Leningrad suburb.

p. 115   *"bridges with broken backs":* the bridges over the river Neva in Leningrad are raised at night to permit the passage of large vessels. See also p. 164 below.

p. 115   the *Shpalernaya:* a street in central Leningrad.

p. 117   *The Return to Ithaca:* the search of Mandelstam's flat is described in the opening chapter of his widow's memoirs, *Hope Against Hope.* Mandelstam was arrested several times during the 1930s, and died in a labor camp at Suchan in December 1938.

p. 117   *peoples' witnesses:* Soviet law required that two parents be present to witness a house search in addition to those under investigation; they were normally press-ganged from among the other occupants of the building.

p. 118   *black raven:* the colloquial term for a police car.

p. 120   *"In Elabuga he didn't soap a noose":* a reference to the poet Marina Tsvetaeva, who hanged herself in the village of Elabuga in 1941. She had returned to the USSR from emigration in 1939; her husband and daughter had been arrested, and she was unable to find literary work.

p. 120   *"In Suchan he didn't run ranting":* a reference to Mandelstam (see above).

p. 120   *Litfond:* Boris Pasternak died in 1960. Though he had been expelled from the Union of Writers as a result of the *Doctor Zhivago* affair, he remained a member of the Litfond, the institution that administers payments to writers.

196

p. 120   *"A snowstorm raged . . ."*: the first stanza of one of the poems from *Doctor Zhivago*.

p. 121   *"The murmur dies . . ."*: the opening lines of Pasternak's poem *Hamlet*, one of the Doctor Zhivago poems that has only recently been published in the USSR.

p. 125   *"Russianante"*: Galich plays with the name of Don Quixote's horse Rosinante, who "had risen from a mean condition to the highest honor a steed could achieve, for it was a cart-horse, and rose to become the charger of a knight-errant."

p. 126   *Arina Rodionovna:* Pushkin's peasant nurse.

p. 126   *Nit gedeige:* (Yiddish) "Don't worry!"

p. 126   *Babii Yar:* the ravine in Kiev where thousands of Jews were murdered by the occupying Nazi troops during the Second World War.

p. 129   *Potma:* the massive labor camp complex in the Mordovian Autonomous Republic.

p. 145   *"Prince Oleg the Wizard . . ."*: the opening lines of Pushkin's historical ballad.

p. 146   *Budenny,* Semen Mikhailovich (1876-1973), Marshal of the Soviet Union, the flamboyant Red cavalry leader during the Civil War.

p. 146   *Babel:* the prose writer Isaac Babel (1894-1941); arrested in 1939, he died in a labor camp.

p. 146   *"Some Marina or other choking"*: the reference is to Marina Tsvetaeva (see above, note to p. 120).

p. 146   *"Some loon in a compound"*: Mandelstam (see above, p. 120). "And I shall never see the famous Phèdre . . .": the opening lines of a lyric by Mandelstam.

p. 149   *"There is no other country that I know"*: a quotation from the Soviet national anthem. The complete second line reads "Where a man can breathe so freely." Composed in 1936 and containing many references to Stalin, the words of the anthem are no longer sung in public.

p. 154   *"You can hardly hear at five paces"*: a reference to Mandelstam's satire on Stalin that led to the poet's arrest in 1934. Mandelstam's poem begins:

> We exist without sensing the land beneath our feet,
> What we say cannot be heard at ten paces,
>
> But where people manage a conversation,
> They mention the mountain-dweller in the Kremlin.

p. 157   *Mtatsminda:* a hill in the center of Tbilisi.

p. 157   *Nina Chavchavadze:* the Georgian wife of the Russian poet and diplomat Alexander Griboedov (1798-1829); soon after their marriage, Griboedov took up a post in Persia, where he was murdered in a riot; the "deathless voice" refers to Nina Chavchavadze's famous epitaph to her husband, to whose memory she remained faithful to the end of her life.

197

p. 164 *Petersburg Romance:* the poem refers at one level to the abortive Decembrist rising of 1825, when a group of young army officers plotted to establish constitutional government in Russia. The rebel troops were drawn up on Senate Square in Petersburg (now called "The Square of the Decembrists"), which is bounded on one side by the buildings of the Senate and Synod.

p. 167 *Alexander Polezhaev:* Russian poet (1804-1838), cashiered, imprisoned and exiled by Tsar Nicholas I for his freethinking verse.

p. 172 *Fame is the Spur:* the epigraph is from Blok's lyric "My Russia, my life, are we to suffer long together" (1910). The Chud' and the Merya are two tribes which in ancient times inhabited an area in the north-east of European Russia.

p. 179 *Serebriany Bor:* "Silver Grove," a riverside area on the western outskirts of Moscow.

p. 180 *Chornaya Rechka:* "The Black Brook," the site of Pushkin's fatal duel in 1837, a wooded area to the north of the contemporary city limits of St. Petersburg.

p. 180 *Tarkhany, Vladimir, Irpen':* small, sleepy provincial towns.

p. 184 *OVIR:* Department of Visas and Registration, the office dealing with residence and visa matters.

p. 187 *Sadovaya Street* is a street in central Moscow.

p. 190 *the Virgin of Kazan* is the most revered of all Russia's ancient icons.

In Which Klim Petrovich Protests

The Ballad of Surplus Value

ri-di-cal)! I was on my hind legs like a sta-lli-on,- Keep it
ne-ver know! Packed my bag-soap and to-wel and un-der-pants, If they

down, for Pete's sake! put a sock in it! It's a sub-ject that a-lways a
kept me I'd not have to go wi-thout! When I got there, my guts were all

tri-cky one, It's not Ma-trea- exist not one bit it ain't! Di-
Pi-u mosso fied, But they -ted me just li-ttle gen-tle-man! Ha-
like a

grace and shame, dis- grace and shame, di- grace and shame! And
ha, clap-clap, ha- ha, clap-clap, ha- ha, clap- clap! But

when I'd near-ly made my name! You've made your name?
I just stood and shut my trap. You've shut your trap?

(4) So whole week from Sun-day to Sun-day night, We were

ha-ving a real-ly fan- tas-tic time, It was Mon-day be-fore I came

back to earth, And I sat down to look at a tell-y show. The ann-

oun-er droned on a-bout pro-gress made In the So- vi-et con-quest of

202